THE PATIENT WHO CURED HIS THERAPIST
and Other Tales of Therapy

THE PATIENT WHO CURED HIS THERAPIST
and Other Tales of Therapy

■

STANLEY SIEGEL
and
ED LOWE, JR.

A DUTTON BOOK

DUTTON
Published by the Penguin Group
Penguin Books USA Inc., 375 Hudson Street,
New York, New York 10014, U.S.A.
Penguin Books Ltd, 27 Wrights Lane,
London W8 5TZ, England
Penguin Books Australia Ltd, Ringwood,
Victoria, Australia
Penguin Books Canada Ltd, 10 Alcorn Avenue,
Toronto, Ontario, Canada M4V 3B2
Penguin Books (N.Z.) Ltd, 182-190 Wairau Road,
Auckland 10, New Zealand

Penguin Books Ltd, Registered Offices:
Harmondsworth, Middlesex, England

First published by Dutton,
an imprint of New American Library,
a division of Penguin Books USA Inc.
Distributed in Canada by McClelland & Stewart Inc.

First Printing, August, 1992
10 9 8 7 6 5 4 3 2 1

REGISTERED TRADEMARK—MARCA REGISTRADA

LIBRARY OF CONGRESS CATALOGING-IN-PUBLICATION DATA

Siegel, Stanley, 1946–
The patient who cured his therapist, and other tales of therapy / Stanley Siegel and
Ed Lowe, Jr.
    p. cm.
ISBN 0-525-93410-3
1. Family psychotherapy—Case studies. 2. Psychotherapist and patient. I. Lowe, Ed,
1946–   . II. Title.
RC488.5.S52 1992   91-43007
616.89′156—dc20   CIP
                                                                                              r92

Printed in the United States of America
Set in Palatino
Designed by Julian Hamer

94-0561 war

to my daughter Alyssa,
from whom I continue
to learn about creativity
STANLEY SIEGEL

and . . .

to Dolores
ED LOWE, JR.

CONTENTS

ACKNOWLEDGMENTS

The authors would like to thank David Hamilton, for his early contributions to the project, especially to the stories, "Sin's Syndrome," and "The Immaculate Misconception"; Nancy Rose, of Levine, Thall and Plotkin, for being at once an agent, a lawyer, and a creative advisor; Alexia Dorszynski, for her editing skills; Ed Delaney, for yet again being in the right place at the right time; Peggy Papp and Olga Silverstein, for their dedication and expertise as teachers and colleagues; and Phyllis Singer and Joey Smith, for their constant encouragement. Thanks also to Katherine Kilgore, Rick Mitz, and Pat and Ben Heller for their advice and criticism; Gary McLoughlin, for his fax machine; and to Bill Ross, for on-the-spot computer wizardry when deadlines loomed, and the hardware balked.

INTRODUCTION

Despite the early hour the thermometer outside registered scant digits below triple figures. Steamy summer moisture clouded the city air. A handsome man wearing a stylish Italian-cut suit—with shirt, tie, highly polished shoes—and a thick woolen multicolored ski hat, approached me in a room of the East 79th Street branch of the New York Public Library and asked quite bluntly if I knew about psychology. He had pulled down the hat to cover his ears. I saw nobody at any other table.

I was deep into my third year as a practicing psychotherapist. Books and papers about psychology were spread out before me like newspapers at a Louisiana crawfish boil. I was busy and did not want to be distracted. Straining to maintain a noncommittal expression, I looked up at the summertime Ski Hat Man.

"Psychology?" I asked blankly. "No, I don't know anything about psychology."

"Well, let me ask you a question, anyway," he nearly bellowed. "Do you think the CIA and the FBI could be monitoring my conversations through my hat somehow? Is that possible?"

Wondering, "Why me?" I answered that although the question struck me as interesting, I didn't know. I nodded toward the research librarian and told the man, "You know, she might be able to help you. She's very good at finding things out."

The man thanked me politely and approached the research librarian's desk.

"Do you think the CIA and the FBI could be monitoring my conversations through my hat?" he asked, pointing to his head.

She must have heard us already, for she had reached for a hefty volume and was placing it on the desk by the time he arrived. "I really don't know offhand," she said, "but we might get some help from this book. It's a directory of federal government agencies. Let me see . . ."

She was not mocking him, and the calmness of her approach to the resource material suggested that she was not merely humoring him, either. It seemed to me that she had decided simply to treat his concern as legitimately as he did and proceed from there. Ashamed of myself, but only slightly, I marveled at her instinct, because I had been half intentionally, half instinctively developing a similar approach to my own work.

The research librarian appeared to be having little success finding answers, but while she perused her book, another man strode to her desk, apologized for interrupting, and then interrupted. "I'm sorry. I overheard your question," he said to the Ski Hat Man. "I hope you don't mind my intruding, but I happen to know that you *are* correct in your suspicions. They *can* do it, and they *do* do it. They've been monitoring my dialogues for years, through my transistor radios, through my television, and even—strange as it may sound—through the buckle in one of my belts!"

"I knew it!" said the Ski Hat Man.

The research librarian held up a slip of paper and said, "I've found some telephone numbers for you, numbers for both agencies, the CIA and the FBI. Here, you can call and ask yourself." The Ski Hat Man took the paper, and the two men wandered off to another room, conversing about the inconveniences of being spied upon.

I felt like applauding. The librarian had responded to an eccentric with the same respect that she might have offered anyone else, and as a result a man not suffering from his illusions had discovered another man not suffering from the same kind of illusions. Presumably, a valuable friendship thus was struck; mutual needs were served; fears were comforted.

Furthermore, it was entirely possible that neither of these two new acquaintances would consider the other's apparent illusions bizarre, problematic, or symptomatic of any mental or emotional disorder, or even consider them illusions. On the contrary, each was gladdened to have encountered the other. They supported each other's point of view. Together they could enjoy a universe that, though different from mine, was quite satisfactory, and one from whose perspective they might even think of my universe as aberrant, strange, unrealistic, illusionary, even neurotic. They were in the process of discovering a new relationship, and the possibilities for its success were limitless. All I knew about them so far was that they complemented each other and supported each other in a way few others could. If a friendship developed out of this chance encounter, it surely would be an exquisite union.

It occurred to me that my work, psychotherapy, was less a way of understanding individuals than of understanding the relationships between people, what brought them together in the first place, what needs and gifts their relationships addressed, what changes they made to accommodate each other; what the origins of their complementary strengths and weaknesses were. After all, much of our idiosyncratic behavior, good or bad, has its origins in the idiosyncrasies of our parents, with whom we had our very first relationships. Much of what we look for in new relationships—friends, lovers, or our children—offers the same kinds of support and even conflict that comforted us in our earliest relationships. *Bizarre, neurotic, crazy,* and *antisocial* are sublimely relative terms, often absolutely unrelated to the function of the accused's behavior. Their meaning depends wholly on the perceptions of somebody else, and the comparative comfort or discomfort their manifestations cause somebody else.

Early in my studies, I discovered that my developing therapeutic aesthetic responded to lectures and literature from followers of what was then considered a new school of thought. With excitement, I immersed myself in the ideas of the pioneers of these theories—Murray Bowen, Carl Whittaker, Jay Haley, Nathan Ackerman—who themselves had rebelled against the tenets of traditional psychotherapy. All of their ideas were loosely gathered beneath the categorical umbrella of Family Systems Therapy, then a catchall phrase for a variety of emerging theories and methods. They shared in common the premise that an individual's problem, rather than being purely dysfunctional, might actually function to support the stability of a relationship, usually within a family. They therefore gave the "problem" a positive connotation and then treated it as part of a relationship system, thus moving away from an individual model. While I was still developing my own ideas, I became attracted to and joined with other students and professionals who felt similarly. I learned about and ultimately embraced the ideas of Salvador Minuchin, a pioneer practitioner and the originator of a family systems model called Structural Family Therapy.

Shortly after attending seminars with Minuchin at the Philadelphia Child Guidance Clinic, I met Peggy Papp, a senior faculty member at the Ackerman Institute for Family Therapy in New York, and began studying with her. A year later, Peggy invited me to join her and Olga Silverstein as a colleague in an innovative research project at Ackerman, organized to develop short-term treatment models, particularly for people with extreme behaviorial symptoms. The protocol on the Brief Therapy Project was a team approach in which one therapist conducted therapy with the family while the other team members monitored from behind the observation mirror. The rooms were connected by a telephone intercom. The observing team members could use it to call in comments, questions, and observations to the therapist interviewing the family.

During the course of a single session, the therapist and team would interrupt the session to discuss the information collected and to agree on an intervention that the therapist would then offer to the family.

One strategy called for the therapist to report to the family that she was in disagreement with her team members. The therapist, in her messages, generally supported and encouraged her family to change, while the other team members reported on the risks and consequences. In this way, the family's dilemma about change were dramatized. Eventually, Peggy Papp named the developing technique ''The Greek Chorus,'' because in Greek tragedies the chorus always predicted the ominous consequences of the players' deeds.

In our second year of working together, Peggy, Olga, and I restructured the technique, so that we would all be present in the consultation room together with the family, each of us representing a previously agreed-upon position on the family's options for change. We reserved this extremely powerful method for use with families who presented extreme and acute symptoms and who reported that they had failed in previous therapy. We obtained legal releases from the members of these families, along with their permission to videotape and study the consultations—not only to facilitate their therapy but for later use in research and in teaching. We used several cases from this project to introduce our Triadic Debate method to an international conference held in New York. We compared our methods with the famed Milan Family Studies Center, renowned for their innovative, paradoxical approach.

During my tenure at the Ackerman Institute, as I grew to become a senior faculty member myself and director of the education program, my earlier ideas solidified and became stamped with my own signature.

My therapeutic role, as I now saw it, was vastly different from that of the traditional psychotherapist. It was not to analyze an individual and somehow repair what we determined were his or her isolated imperfections. From a family systems perspective, none of it was isolated; no behavior existed out of context.

My role was to understand the relationships between or among people, to find out how they influenced each other's actions, served each other's needs, complemented each other's strengths, and then teach these same people what they had revealed to me. Even individuals who approached me with what they perceived were personal emotional problems had relationships in their pasts that had profoundly influenced their behavior and their reactions to their present and future reality. They might be honoring a filial legacy, clinging to a stabilizing tradition, freezing a moment in time, or creating an illusion that transcended time and postponed a departure from a family loyalty. If they knew and appreciated the past origins of their reactions to their reality, they could choose new reactions to change their present. If people in apparently troubled relationships were dissatisfied, I could learn what had satisfied them in the first place, what emotional debts they might have incurred to achieve stability, and I could identify the possible opportunities for change and acknowledge the risks involved.

For example, a man and woman meet, learn about each other, and fall in love. They are attracted by each other's positive characteristics; they want to serve each other's needs, encourage and appreciate each other's strengths, assist each other, complement each other. To this end, for the good of each other, they make a dramatic change in their lives; they form a union intended to be permanent, a relationship based on trust, honor, loyalty, and generosity. The change has initial consequences that may be relatively easy to adapt to, and later, long-term consequences that may present more difficulty. In forming the relationship, they develop patterns for protecting the relationship while still preserving their individual integrity; methods emerge for regulating distance and closeness, and the methods create new consequences that one day may be viewed as problems rather than solutions—when they have a child, for instance. Regarding the nurturing and education of the child, each parent is equipped with lessons learned and loyalties forged in different families, perhaps from different group loyalties, different ethnic, economic, cultural, religious, and social traditions. They may disagree, each for the good of the child, each out of loyalty to a different past. The child grows to perceive the conflict and, consciously or otherwise, alters her behavior or changes her life to soothe it or to postpone any feared negative consequences. Maybe she becomes chronically ill, thus drawing attention away from the conflict. Maybe she misbehaves or fails in school, thus achieving a smokescreen dilemma to distract potential combatants and stabilize the family. Mired in her apparent failure or chronic illness, the family then consults a therapist. If the therapist understands the origins of the conflict and knows the foundations of the relationships, he will see that the "problems" may be solutions and the "failures," achievements.

I realized that people who came to therapy already had changed their lives to accommodate the sharp turns and sudden twists that life's milestones can create, and which can destabilize relationships. After making a series of such changes to avoid instability, we sometimes find we have created a new instability. Eventually we may forget that our original intent was honorable and generous, as the consequences of our adaptations are accompanied by unexpected guests—more consequences. The therapist who can find the way back to our motives for the changes we have made might also be able to offer a prescription for embracing different options, different changes that produce the same stabilizing results—but without dishonoring the past that motivated us initially. After learning the origins of a person's behavior, my next challenge was to summon the imagination to offer creative alternatives for change.

My approach to psychotherapy, therefore, started from the premise that we already are all right, or are merely striving to return to being all right; that rather than trying to suppress our powerful, aggressive urges, we are constantly trying to repair wounds we might have suffered, always with the hope of returning to our noblest ideal selves; that negative or crazy behavior is often founded in honorable pursuits. I thought that our admiration of heroic self-sacrifice was a natural human inclination.

I found the positive nature of the approach to be personally fulfilling, even exhilarating. I had long suspected, both intellectually and emotionally, that humans are more inclined (however slightly) toward generosity than they are toward acquisitiveness; more charmed by each other's integrity than they are impressed by clever duplicity; more prone to self-sacrifice than to destructive invasion; more covetous of genuine joy than of momentary satisfaction. I think we like our heroes more than we like our villains because we are motivated in our daily meanderings by a patently human need to be more heroic, to behave better toward each other, generation after generation; and ultimately to improve on the behavior of our ancestors, while trying to remain loyal to such lessons as they learned and tried to pass on. This view of psychotherapy is a way to confirm that suspicion and apply it practically.

Generally speaking, I first detect how a problem functions within a relationship and introduce a new definition of the problem, describing what it accomplishes. Next, I identify and articulate the possible consequences of change, often using the elements of surprise, direct intervention, and even homework as techniques. Dramatizing the dilemma in these ways suggests what possible futures without the problem might be like. Because my approach is active and directive, as well as respectful, the length of therapy is often appreciably shorter than with other kinds of therapy.

Over time three categories—three kinds of matrices of problem-solution combinations that entangled people and distracted them from better enjoying their lives—emerged. Thus, this book is divided into three sections, with stories that illustrate my approach, my discoveries, and I hope, my appreciation of and affection for the human being.

The section called "Exquisite Unions" includes four stories about people who, like the two spied-upon men in the library, manage to find each other, and to find in each other the perfectly, almost mystically complementary attributes that allow us to fulfill each other. One couple, in "Final AIDS," is gay. In "The Immaculate Misconception" we find that an exquisitely matched married couple has agreed to sacrifice a fundamental human need, to abdicate a divine as well as a natural right, for the integrity of their incredible relationship. In "Double Cross," a betrothed man's apparently bizarre behaviorial problem is discovered to have generously spared his fiancée from a perfectly conventional kind of heartache; and in "Jingle Jangle," a typically repetitive marital fight keeps a family true to the histories of its members.

Failure, another sublimely relative characterization, often serves the needs of a relationship. I have seen clear evidence that children sometimes misbehave or, say, fail in school, despite superior intelligence and great talent, because subconsciously they are sacrificing themselves for the good of their immediate family. One young boy I encountered somehow consistently thwarted the curative effects of a medication irrefutably proven to reverse his condition and end his suffering. His very physiology fought the medicine, and he remained chronically ill. How? Why?

By ominous coincidence, which was no coincidence at all, we discovered that the boy's parents' attentions were focused on his illness and not on their own deteriorating marriage. Within the family organism the boy, having discovered that his illness could keep the family together, had assumed the role of attention-getter. When everybody in the family became aware of the sacrificial function of his illness and then paid some attention to repairing the marriage, or at least resolving its dilemma, the boy began to respond to the medicine and recovered completely.

Hence, a section of this book is called "Achieving Failure," showing people who achieve failure because this allows them to achieve functional goals essential to their relative well-being.

Looking at someone's behavior as probably positively functional is automatically more respectful of the person herself, and I have long been drawn to that view. Sometimes its results are quite surprising. In the story that gives the book its title, "The Patient Who Cured His Therapist," I intervened in a case wherein a fellow professional was completely frustrated by her patient's uncommunicative behavior. After a short time I found myself admiring the patient and wondering instead about the intensity of the therapist's frustration. My re-focusing was based on appreciating him and sympathizing with her, my emphasis less on curing than on learning first, then revealing what I had learned. My approach assumed that the uncommunicative patient probably was acting in his own best interest and—for what reasons I would try to learn and understand—not that he was behaving badly and ought to have corrected himself.

In "Getting Crazy," a woman described as a societal failure engaged regularly, and at the risk of going to jail, in what I eventually called "responsible shoplifting." In the eyes of the professional therapeutic community, she was a failure. Well-meaning counselors had advised her for years to stop shoplifting because, they said, such behavior was crazy and irresponsible.

I saw the situation from a different perspective. Given her family history, I considered her too responsible and not crazy enough. Furthermore, I thought I heard in her story the possible answer to her dilemma, a solution that honored her past. The choice to change her life's direction was hers.

In "Holocaused," three grown children conspire to achieve failure, one more spectacularly than the other, as a means of protecting their parents' marriage while simultaneously adhering to the messages of their ancestral families. When they are taught to view their failures as functional, as loyal, even as generous and loving behavior, they are freed to control the extent to which they choose to continue to fail. They can allow themselves success. But—again, emphasizing the consequences of change—my colleagues and I recognized that although change would liberate the members of a younger generation who had thus far failed and suffered for the family's history and stability, the cost of such change would be borne by the older generation. Would they pay? Would their children let them pay? We had to point out the options and let the family decide.

Finally, in "The Wall of Sheets," I tell how my cotherapist and I fared, in a long and frustrating series of sessions with a married couple whose ancestral loyalties were so strong, so honored, so deeply rooted, that they had created a sustained failure in their relationship. The continuance of the failure defined the relationship itself. The failure was crucial to the relationship. We needed months to recognize it, and moments to honor it.

Bluntly put, I'm not interested in restructuring psyches. I'm interested in how a person can see his structure, his history, and his loyalties, and do something about the lessons they teach, if need be, or to accept and appreciate them, if not.

I see therapy as art, as an extremely subjective art, too, collaborative and communicative between the therapist and his client—two human beings, one with tremendous experience with his own troubles, the other supposedly possessing vast knowledge of other people's troubles, not to mention their statistically recorded patterns and clinical names.

In a way, the process sometimes seems as simple as the cliché that requires walking a mile in the other person's moccasins before judging her behavior or advising her that she must change it. If a therapist can learn, understand, and then absorb a person's culture so that he can truly empathize—walk the mile in her moccasins—the therapist is much better equipped to assist her in rewriting her own story. Looking at the science as an art, therapy for me is as personally involving as creating a painting, or, better yet, as singing in harmony, its turns and maneuvers as much an expression of my own personal aesthetic as the patient's problems most probably reflect her own. If I accept the patient's problem not as pathology, not even as fact, but as simply her story, I can both react to the story—share its sadness or its frustration—and engage, in concert with her, toward the purpose of helping rewrite the story, change its direction, create a new narrative.

Thus, the stories in the third section, "Transcending Illusions," illustrate the extent to which a therapist tries to become involved in entering another's universe. Illusions that often seem out of context sometimes require that the therapist participate in them, even join them, before the context is discovered. They seem to be disconnected sometimes, but clinical research repeatedly shows their undeniable connections to past relationships. In one of the "Spaghetti Stories," I try and try and try to find the connection, not knowing what I'm looking for or how to go about it. I never learn the purpose of the illusion, but I do learn that it serves a purpose, because the patient so ardently protects and controls it. In the other "Spaghetti Story," I again don't learn the context, but by honoring the illusions, I discover a way for the person to manage them, control them better, function with them. In "Sin's Syndrome," the illusion more obviously serves the needs of a relationship, protects loyalty to an honorable code of conduct, and establishes an ironic fidelity to a family unit—but it is a solution whose consequences can become desperately costly. In "Father Knows Best," the illusion of one member's culpability is accepted by the entire family in the interest of protecting another member who is not yet ready to accept her responsibility.

My hope is that stories like those in this volume help show an entirely different view of relationships, give a new perspective on apparently problematic behavior, on so-called failures among members of couples, families, extended families, and even communities, because so often such problems represent noble, generous, and positive self-sacrifice on the part of the symptomatic members.

In such one-session stories as "The Immaculate Misconception," "Getting Crazy," and "The Patient Who Cured His Therapist," the therapeutic stages—respect, involvement, inspiration, intervention, and, sometimes, magic—merge perfectly to create new stories. In stories of more extended, multi-session therapy, such as "Jingle Jangle," "Double Cross," and particularly "Holocaused," the process of discovery is more cumulative, though no less exquisite, and the stories extended to novella complexity.

The Patient Who Cured His Therapist is intended to illustrate those discoveries about relationships that I have found so exciting and rewarding during the past twenty years, to offer their example as possible alternatives for people, and to provide the reader with amusing, compelling, entertaining, and enlightening true stories, gleaned from my memory, my notes, and my videotaped recordings of sessions with patients.

Each of the three categories, "Exquisite Unions," "Achieving Failure," and "Transcending Illusions," illustrates manifestations of my view. Each story, in its own way, illuminates the fundamental positiveness of my view, an attribute I hope the recalling and retelling of these stories someday will make contagious.

—STANLEY SIEGEL
New York
June 1991

THE STORIES IN THIS BOOK ALL ARE TRUE AND HAPPENED when they are identified as having happened. To protect the confidentiality of the patients, however, the authors have changed the names of all patients and practitioners directly involved in the therapy sessions depicted in the stories. For the same reason, patients' occupations and some places and circumstances have been changed, as well, requiring some alteration and therefore fictionalization.

EXQUISITE
UNIONS

■

True love may be just exactly as our most saccharine, violin-accompanied, Disney-animated fantasies envision it; and the more cynical members of the psychotherapeutic community ought to hear—at least once, anyway—the chord that the image never fails to strike in us.

People are not drawn to each other exclusively for selfish reasons—say, to satisfy personal longings, serve insatiable libidos, or even to perpetuate their genetic components through reciprocal altruism—although all these goals fit into the love equation. But as a species we also share a fundamental need to respect, honor, and give; to complement weaknesses with strengths; to teach; to be loyal; to achieve harmony and balance and then share its comforts.

As the stories in this section attest, behavior that appears to be selfish often emerges as self-sacrificial when examined in the lights of a more positive premise. What appears to be a problem turns out to be a beautiful and generous bond, and, in fact, not a problem at all but a solution.

Sometimes the solution is sacred, as in "The Immaculate Misconception," wherein a couple sacrifices their sexuality for their spirituality, or "Final AIDS," in which a gay couple heroically serves each other's greatest needs, one in the present, one in the past. Sometimes the solutions appear comparatively bizarre, as in "Double Cross." And sometimes they are painfully typical, as in "Jingle Jangle," a story in which a repetitive fight keeps a family true to the histories of its members.

The undying marvel is that we continue to find each other, to consciously and subconsciously discover the characteristics, gifts, and needs in each other that we can draw from and add to, in what appears to be an indomitable need to positively influence our reality.

THE
IMMACULATE
MISCONCEPTION

ACCORDING TO CONVENTIONAL ASSUMPTIONS, TRADITION-
ally, therapy takes time. Either the therapist only gradually
discerns the real issues behind the "patient's" apparent
problems, or the "patient" is slow or reluctant to shift her
focus from the security of her old problems to the uncer-
tainties of change.

I maintain, however, that therapy can be as sudden
and powerful a thunderbolt as a death or a birth in the
family, immediately changing every participant's life forever. I cannot say how frequently the opportunity may
arise for such therapeutic explosiveness, but I can attest
to the fact that such opportunities do arise. I have
seized and capitalized on them, as I did in the case of
Steven and Nancy Bembridge, when I also violated the
unwritten code of therapeutic neutrality by thrusting
myself—bodily, as it turned out—into their perceived
problem.

Long Island, 1976

I glanced briefly at the slip of paper identifying the Bembridge couple. I knew that an adoption agency had referred

them to me. The agency had denied their application to adopt, but I had no idea why.

Opening my office door to greet them, I was struck instantly by the image they presented against the soothing but bland backdrop of our fairly large, mostly beige waiting room. They were seated together—fiercely together—in the middle of a long wooden, pew-like bench. They seemed to be joined—Krazy-Glued—at the hips, thighs, and triceps. Mrs. Bembridge wore a black blouse and a white skirt; her husband wore a white shirt and black slacks. A perfect checkerboard pattern. I wondered if they realized.

They rose together. He was taller than she. They seemed uncomfortable, but then, almost everybody does in the initial encounter. We shook hands.

After introducing myself, I motioned them to enter the office. They strode through the door together, made for the couch opposite my chair, and sank together into the middle of the too-soft sofa. The cushions on either side of them billowed, pressing them even closer together than before, if that were possible.

I tried not to stare. I was caught somewhere between awe and admiration, at the moment focusing perhaps all too much on awe. If I can exaggerate the image only slightly, they presented a picture of Siamese penguins, dwarfed by a huge white, glacial background.

I gazed at them as if they were in a painting, and the picture triggered thoughts about my own background. For much of my youth, and throughout my undergraduate days, I had wanted to be a painter. In looking back at my sculptures and paintings from those days, I notice that all my work focused almost exclusively on the space between people, the proximity or distance between them. Artists call the space between people or objects "negative space," although it always captured my eye the same way other elements of a picture did.

Perhaps because I was born with vision in one eye only, I view the world differently. For me, negative space always was just as real as so-called positive space, showing what separated us from each other as well as what drew us near. The consciousness of imagery, and that specific focus as well, stayed with me and became a prominent part of my inner machinery for examining relationships—but never so graphically as when I gazed at the Bembridges.

I thus began sort of distractedly, even amateurishly. "So, why have you come to see me?"

Nancy Bembridge answered tersely and distinctly: "We were referred by an adoption agency," she said. "We wanted to adopt a baby, and we went to see them about it, and they said no." Then she demurred, saying, "Well, nobody actually gets turned down that quickly by an agency. It's just that they said that maybe we should see someone instead."

I still had no clue. "Why would they refuse to give you a baby?" I asked. "I mean, if that's what they were saying."

"Well, it isn't because we don't have a nice home," she said with convincing certainty. "We have a nice home, okay? With a big yard, three bedrooms, a guest room, and a room for a child. We have a good income, more than enough. I work. Steven works. And we come from good backgrounds, both of us. We both grew up in the church, so there's no problem in the background. And we both have our health. No medical problems. We have a dog . . ."

She continued, but talking more to Steven than to me, which was fine because, on the surface anyway, I was already pretty much convinced, and her behavior allowed me to gaze longer at this painting they presented. When she paused, searching for more items for the litany, I interrupted:

"That's a lot of good reasons for them to give you a baby. How did they explain why they wouldn't give you a baby?"

"Well," she said carefully, staring into her husband's eyes with a strangely powerful expression of combined devotion and resignation, "we've been married six years, and we haven't had sexual intercourse. And I guess they don't like that.''

She looked down. A heartbreaking expression of shame crossed her face. His expression suddenly mirrored hers.

For a second I had to check my reaction.

I had been and still was fascinated by the way their bodies were welded together. The shock of their confession was mitigated by an equally sudden recognition of the message in their imagery. Of course they didn't engage in sexual intercourse. They were stuck together, hip to hip. Unless humans were reinvented wearing their reproductive apparatus like sidearms, procreation would be impossible. These two had not left each other's side long enough to allow their genitalia the courtesy of even a polite introduction. They were fused.

I realized that where I normally see the space between people, I had seen fusion, and the fusion was their solution to some problem. I didn't know the problem yet, but recognizing their solution triggered a whole new program of thoughts and ideas—about melding, about clinging, about the good and bad results of varying degrees of separation. What was their sexual abstention a solution to?

And what would happen if somebody or something found its way between them? Would they then be forced to reveal what they were so desperately protecting?

I knew that somehow I had to understand the meaning of their fusion. I decided to take a huge risk—to challenge it directly.

"Adopt *me*," I said brightly, as if I had suddenly discovered the solutions to everyone's problems, theirs and mine. I rose.

They had made sure there would be no room for a child to exist between them. There was no room for anything at all between them, not air, not the initial separation required to initiate sexual intercourse, not anything. I wanted to see what would happen if something or someone did appear between them. How would the picture change? This was radical intervention by any standards, mainly because of its suddenness, partly because of my very personal intrusion, but an action measured to equal the intensity of the situation.

I moved toward the couch. "You want a child to love?" I asked. "Then I'll be your baby." As I approached them, Steven eyed me with the widened pupils of a squirrel encountering cats.

Together they froze. Some flicker in their stunned expression, some punctuation in their body language, still reassured me that I was probing the right place, and with precisely the right instrument. It was as if I couldn't see, but I knew where I was going.

"I had a terrible childhood," I said, pressing, moving closer, aiming directly at the nonexistent space between them, determined to pry it open. "I don't remember anything nice about it. My mommy and daddy didn't want me around. They never kissed me. They never hugged me. All they did was scream at me all the time. I missed being a baby. I want to be a baby somebody wants!"

I literally burrowed between them, shouldering my way into the non-space. I should probably point out here that I am slight of build. I accomplished the burrowing without any complicating difficulties, although it must have looked bizarre.

"You want a baby?" I said when I'd pried them apart. "I'll be your baby.

"Mommy?" I nestled in Nancy's shoulder. "Daddy?" I turned and murmured plaintively, summoning an expression as close as I could conjure to a puppy's.

"Mommy?" I asked, returning my gaze to Nancy. "Give me a kiss, Mommy. Show me how you want to love your baby, Mommy."

Nancy began to weep. Steven was taut as harp strings.

I turned and leaned on his shoulder. "Hug me, Daddy, please? Please . . . ?"

Steven's reaction was violent. He leaned forward, fists

clenched, knuckles pressed into his forehead. "How can you *do* this?" he demanded angrily. "We came here for help! I never heard of such a thing! You push yourself . . . your problems . . . you throw your problems at us? This is unheard of! This is unbelievable! It's ridiculous! You . . . you . . . God damn!"

He stood and stomped toward the door. Nancy rose and followed, as if tethered. Steven was shouting as he grasped the doorknob. He clenched it, twisted it menacingly, and howled again, "We came here for help!"

There have been moments in my life when I wished I were not so slight and unthreatening, moments when I wished I could rise from my theater seat to a full six-foot-six height and stare down a potential antagonist, but this was not one of them. As outrageous as it may now seem, I pulled my knees and curled myself to become as small as possible: I cocked my head sideways to a nearly coquettish angle and keened in my softest, most supplicant voice:

"You're abandoning me," I chirped. "You haven't even adopted me yet, and you're abandoning me!"

The room spun on my word choice.

The Bembridges became statues. The echo of *abandoning me* hung like smoke trapped inside a jar. The solemnity was terrifying. After heart-stopping seconds, Steven's face contorted. His upper body shuddered once, trembled, and he crumbled into sobs. Somehow *Abandoning me* was key.

Nancy looked at me. I rose respectfully and stood. She escorted her husband back to the couch. They returned to their welded position. Steven composed himself. For a few long moments we said nothing. The moment for magic was over and the work about to begin. I waited for one of them to speak.

Eventually, Steven started:

"As a baby, I was left on the steps of a church. St. Leonard's Church. In a basket. Obviously, I don't know much about it. I don't remember much of what I learned, except that it *was* a basket. Wicker. Not a cardboard box." He hesitated. "It doesn't matter. The details don't matter." He hesitated again. "It had a blanket, the basket. A blue blanket. Nuns at the orphanage always told me that it was a blue blanket and that it was wrapped tightly around me. I was left in the fall, but they said on a warm day. The nuns took care of me into high school."

Steven sat erect on the couch, hands on his knees, eyes cast downward, occasionally glancing up and into Nancy's eyes. I bit into my forefinger, thinking about the details that didn't matter: a basket, not a cardboard box; a blue blanket, for a son; and wrapped around him on an autumn day that was warm. Each detail suggested that his mother had loved him despite what she had done: abandoned him.

"I was lucky," he insisted. "I was taught how to live a good life, and I got a good start. Lucky. I mean it, too. I had a place to live, some work to do, a school to go to, someone who cared, someone who made you do your work—your homework, your work in the yard, whatever. They cared enough about you to make sure you grew up right, ate your meals, and did your jobs. Everyone always says, 'Poor orphans!' but I got a good education, someone who cared, a bed, three meals a day, the chance to grow up without a struggle; and I got a good start in life." Despite Steven's gratitude his underlying sorrow was obvious.

"How was it," I interrupted, "that you and Nancy met?"

"We met at a party," he answered, his head rising and his face slowly yielding to a smile. He extended his arms the way a bishop might, acknowledging the affection of a throng of disciples.

"I saw it right away," he said. "She was everything I imagined a woman could be. Meeting her, knowing her, getting to know her, falling in love. I thought I'd found everything I'd missed. In her I found everything I lost. I got it all back."

He gazed at her beatifically. She stared back in rapt adoration. "I never loved a woman before," he said, his eyes still locked on hers. "She was . . . perfect. All of a sudden

I didn't even have to think, and she was there. If I wanted to go for a walk, she would say, 'I have an idea: let's go for a walk.' If I just wanted to lay my head on her shoulder, she was there. If she wanted to go shopping, it was at a time I was in the mood to go shopping. If she asked, 'Do you love me?' she asked at exactly the time I was thinking, 'I love her so much!' If I felt like I wanted a sandwich, she would say, 'You want a sandwich?' Plus, we liked the same TV shows, you know? *Hawaii Five-O, The Flying Nun, Dragnet.* We went to bed at the same time—ten-thirty. We got up at the same time—eight. She liked blue and hated orange, you know? Bologna and American cheese on Wonder Bread, with Miracle Whip. Can you believe it? With tomato soup? For lunch? Now, how many people like that?" We chuckled.

"She seemed to know everything about me before I told her. She's always been just . . . just about everything you could ask for. Just about . . . perfect."

I let ten seconds hang, and then asked Nancy: "What about you, Nancy? What about when you met Steven?"

"Oh, it was really a dance," she said, sighing. "At the high school. The spring formal." She looked directly at Steven. "He was a perfect dancer."

"What did you tell him about yourself?"

"Well, that I kind of grew up by myself. That was the most important part. So I was ready, you know, for responsibility. Mom and Dad both worked all day, and that meant somebody had to take care of the house. And that was me. I'm the oldest, so I got used to running things. You know: three young kids, my brothers and sisters. Before I knew anything else, I knew how to get everything fixed up so that they could go off to school and get back home without any problems."

Every evening, she said, her mother returned home from work before her father, but exhausted most of the time, and so she relied on Nancy to help the other kids with homework, baths, dinner, nurturing, encouragement, not to mention ironing, dusting, and general cleaning. "Sometimes," said Nancy, "I felt as if the whole house would fall apart if I wasn't there. We—the kids—would make the meal and clean up, and Mom would go sit in the front room and then go to bed. The whole family'd go to Mass on Sunday, of course, but not until after I got the kids dressed. And we'd run back afterward to make dinner. I cooked. My sister helped set the table. Dad and Mom took a nap in the afternoon. Church and dinner were the only times each week they were with the family.

"Then they were grown, the kids," she said with finality.

"So, when I met Steven, he was so, like, comfortable. It was so easy to fix things for him. He appreciated things so much. You could do the wash, and he would say, 'Thank you.' Or, you know, make a dinner or whatever. He was just so sweet. Whatever I did for him, just fold the towels the right way or whatever. It's always been so good to be with him.

"You know, the work is not so different from the kids," she said. "The laundry's the same, the meals, the house, the dusting and things, but he just appreciates it so much. It's just so comfortable with him. He cares. I take care of him, and he cares so much. Even after eight years he still says, 'Thank you' after every meal. Seriously, he says, 'Thank you,' after every meal."

She paused. She grinned at him and looked down, blushing.

I sat in wonderment at what they had accomplished. It was not the first time I had encountered people whose unique needs served each other with so perfect a fit, but I continue to marvel that they always seem to gravitate toward and eventually discover each other. What appeared to be a problem—what would be defined by most people as a problem, and what *was* defined as a problem by the adoption agency—was actually their solution, and a heroic one at that. I was amazed, and I wanted to tell them that and why; but also I was aware that in telling them, in pointing out what they had accomplished, I would be delivering the very tool that could change their perfect solution. Knowing what they had done would enable them to choose to undo it.

I paused for a moment and said with near reverence, "It's very difficult for me to put into words the respect I feel for both of you and for the extraordinary union you have created. Yours appears to be a higher order of marriage than the norm. I know you have been made to feel wrong for having been married all these years without consummating the marriage, but I think you have been misunderstood. Your needs, each of you, are unique, given your unusual histories. Your way of satisfying them is also unique. Most people would not have had the strength to take care of each other and protect each other, in the face of convention, the way you have."

They had sacrificed their sexuality to serve each other's needs. How could I say that?

I looked at Steven. "As you said yourself," I told him, "in Nancy you have regained everything that you lost, found everything you longed for. Clearly, and it must be clear to you, she is more than a woman to you, more than a wife. She is also a mother. In fact, a Madonna. You have found the woman who, if she had nothing else in the world, if she had no hope, would have managed to find a blue blanket and a basket for you, and wrapped you tight, and put you on the steps of the best place on the best day. I don't know *how* you found her. I mean, it's almost a miracle. But here you are. I'll bet sometimes you don't believe it yourself, right?"

Steven shrugged and grinned in agreement. I looked at Nancy.

"And you found in Steven a child of your own, a son you could care for in exactly the ways you learned in your own family, exactly the ways that made you feel important and needed and fulfilled. Plus, he gives you love openly and willingly in return for your care. He is your perfect child.

You have what parents ache for, long for, and never feel that they get: appreciation for their devotion. Look at what you've made here! This is a beautiful, totally unselfish arrangement. Your love for each other transcends the way we usually think of marriage.

"I understand why you would not have intercourse in this marriage. It would be a violation of the sacred pact you have made with each other. It would jeopardize everything. Steven, if you were to have sex with Nancy, it would diminish her. She would become an ordinary woman, less than your Madonna, and you would be in danger of losing once again everything you had regained. Similarly, Nancy, if you had sex with Steven, he would become an ordinary man, and you would lose the perfect son you have found, the child who needs you so much and so appreciates you and loves you for caring for him. In a very real and important way, given the nature of your relationship, making love with him would amount to incest.

"Would a child change your arrangement profoundly? Irrevocably? Certainly. Maybe that is another reason why you haven't risked creating a child. Think of it this way: you have been acting in the best interests of your relationship and of each other. When it's no longer in your best interests to act that way, maybe you will change your arrangement, whatever the risks."

There followed a church-like silence. The paradox was clear; so was the dilemma of change. The price of change would rest squarely on their shoulders.

We shook hands with a quiet, firm enthusiasm, knowing that in a microscopic, fleeting way, we had grown fond of each other, would never forget each other, were forever altered by our meeting. I said, "Listen, you are generous and caring people. You know that, I know that. I'm proud to have met you. Call anytime, if you decide to. My best to you."

They left, just as glued together as they had arrived.

Two years later, I received a birth announcement in the

mail for Gerald Steven Bembridge. I had a bizarre reaction to the card, which I still have. I keep it as a symbol, another reminder of the cliché that things are not always what they seem. My initial burst of joy—a natural reaction at the news of a birth—was cut short by the image of how much room Nancy and Steven Bembridge had had between them. None. Where would a child fit into these lives?

Given what they had told me about their backgrounds and life together, it struck me that they had changed their arrangement drastically, and I wondered what the consequences would be. Maybe, once they had accepted themselves and stopped feeling guilty or negative, they had felt better prepared to change. But maybe they were yielding again to such outside pressure as they felt to be acceptable.

For them, I thought, a baby really was a mixed blessing, and I did not know whether they would be able to deal with it.

Nor did I ever hear from them again.

POSTSCRIPT

The process of coupling generally begins with a courtship in which partners display their talents and strengths in an effort to attract each other. Gradually, they solidify the relationship by revealing their fears and weaknesses and appealing to each other's compassion and desire to be needed—always with the risk of rejection and abandonment.

In the case of the Bembridges, this theme acted as the centerpiece of their relationship, exaggerated by opposite but complementary histories and decidedly unconventional histories at that. They so feared abandonment that they were willing, and proved able, to sacrifice the most powerful and urgent means of communicating their feelings—sexual intercourse—to protect themselves from the realization of their worst fears. Not yet knowing that, I began with the simple premise that we cannot judge without knowing the context. Behavior so unusual and self-sacrificial as theirs must have stemmed from an equally unusual and powerful set of circumstances.

My two interventions—wedging myself between them, first, and then accusing Steven of abandoning me—might seem to have come out of the blue, but they did not. That is not to say that my responses were calculated or that a model for them could be found in any textbook I had read. Arising from a state of such intense concentration, my actions are often as much the result of intuition as they are of clinical experience, and I too am taking a risk. With the Bembridges, I was listening to their words and simultaneously absorbing whole paragraphs of their non-verbal communication: the imagery in their adherence to each other, their identical though inverted mode of dress, their stories of intense mutuality. All of it strongly suggested a fear of separation, an inability to be apart. Those undeniable suggestions steered me into a mental process that included my imagining what it would mean to me to be in that situation and what in my personal and professional experiences seemed most comparable to their experience.

I was led to two conclusions: first, that a couple so glued to each other had to have organized themselves around a fear of abandonment; and, secondly, that words alone would not be enough to dislodge them from the stronghold they had created.

Despite my own fear of taking a radical action, an action comparable to performing risky surgery, I knew my response had to measure up to their extreme situation. I knew my action would be unconventional. I could only hope that their reaction would be to reveal the meaning of their dilemma in some more obvious way. I drew upon my own memories of fears of abandonment—we all have suffered varying degrees of panic over the possibility of being abandoned—and, however minor my experiences had been by comparison to the Bembridges, they turned out to be in the right category. Once dramatized, the dilemma unfolded. Did they really want a third party in their exquisitely balanced arrangement? Could they balance their desire for a family life against their fears of disruption and abandonment? Only they could answer; only they could decide. Either way, there would be consequences, and they either would cope with the consequences or perhaps return. Children are a mixed blessing for any couple, because of the range of the joy and sorrows in raising a child. Here, the balance of the relationship, joys and sorrows notwithstanding, would be threatened by the mere presence of a child. For the Bembridges, this one session made that recognition dramatically stark. We parted recognizing the dilemma and knowing that their responsibility was to make a decision.

Over the years, I have come to believe that the length of therapy depends on the time it takes to identify or redefine a problem. The rate at which I proceed depends on a number of variables: my ability to understand the context of the problem, the stubbornness of the reality that the family constructs around the problem-symptom to maintain stability, and the time it takes for all of us to construct a new definition that allows the family to solve the underlying problem without the original symptom as a centerpiece—assuming they choose to face whatever consequences that would entail. They may, after all, choose to keep the symptom rather than face the unknown consequences.

Like with a family physician, I may have periodic involvement with a family over an extended time. When they reach a particular impasse, the family may choose to return for a consultation in an attempt to understand the dilemmas that help maintain the new impasse. I prefer this model of therapy to other, long-term models that require continuous, regularly scheduled involvement.

Of course, when there is great suffering and pain or a severe developmental delay because a family is at an impasse for a long time, they may benefit from ongoing support and guidance as the consequences of change unfold. In those cases I stay with the clients and help them to develop guideposts to refer to when the therapy ends. But in most cases, the family that summons the creativity to organize a problem-solution combination requiring therapy in the first place will continue to act creatively in its own interests, whenever therapy ends.

FINAL AIDS

I WAS TEACHING FAMILY THERAPY AT THE UNIVERSITY OF CALifornia at Berkeley and working with the AIDS Project at a medical hospice in San Francisco. My job, in collaboration with the visiting nurses, was to deal with the staff, the physicians, their patients, the patients' survivors, and their families. The issues were bereavement, the anticipation of death, and the patients, who before dying were demonstrating psychological problems that were damaging their relationships with their loved ones and making the inevitable lonelier for all concerned.

All of the cases were tragic; all of the work left scars. All the players, in their way, were unforgettable. If I had to select one story, representative of the heroism of a community under siege, one that managed to reflect their hope and optimism despite the bleakest of circumstance, I would choose easily the story based on the case of a man I shall call Martin Miller.

San Francisco, Winter 1987

A nurse referred the case to me. She had been treating Martin at home for three years in his struggle against certain deterioration. The local health community preferred to treat AIDS patients at home for as long as possible, and I think it was a wise and humane course. Martin had by this time an advanced case of Kaposi's sarcoma, the cruel cancer most specifically common to AIDS patients. He also had pneumosistis pneumonia, another classic AIDS-related problem.

He was deep into the final stages.

The nurse referred Martin to me because he had attempted suicide and failed. She was stunned into a nervous stupefaction more by Martin's failure, it seemed to me, than by his attempt; suicide was by no means an unheard-of course of self-treatment in that place at that time.

Like many AIDS sufferers who have reached the end of their tolerance for agony, Martin had swallowed a "death cocktail," a morphine-based concoction of four different poisons, any one of which should have dispatched him to eternity the moment it touched his lips. I have suspected since our first encounter that the nurse's befuddled awe regarding Martin's survival was based on a more extensive knowledge of events leading up to the apparent miracle than was prudent for her to reveal.

Traditionally in these "cocktail" cases the visiting nurse tended the bar. Being closest to the patient for the longest hours, she was at once the likeliest of her care-providing colleagues to be so compassionate, and also the best able to procure the most effectively lethal spirits quietly. Traditionally, not wanting to make any mistakes or cause any more suffering than the unimaginable suffering they already had seen endured, those who mixed the "death cocktails" were generous in their pouring.

Also, like many of the nursing personnel I met during that sustained, heartbreaking period of my life, this particular nurse was sufficiently inclined toward spirituality to suspect, and to suggest quite frankly to me, that Martin had somehow kept himself alive—however unwittingly or subconsciously—because he had some unfinished business, though he may not have known exactly what it was. In fact, she thought my value was that I might be able to help him define what it was, so he could take care of it and then, of course, die.

Respecting her premise at least for the moment, I visited Martin Miller and his lover, Tyrone Weeks, at their ironically cheery, colorful Victorian house on one of the hills in the Castro District of San Francisco, an almost exclusively gay community not far from the Haight. They lived in an apartment in the back of the house, accessible by a private gate and a cement path lined with calla lilies—long-stemmed, bell-shaped white flowers that were as welcoming as they were sensuous. The living room of the apartment faced a tiny garden out back, and Martin's hospital bed, which dominated the room, allowed him to face that way, too. Their word processors stood as sentinels flanking the window on the garden. Martin was a novelist-scriptwriter; Tyrone wrote copy for small advertising businesses.

Martin was, in a word, wretched. His internal organs were scarred and his skin blotched with purple sores. He was frail, disfigured, gaunt—the very image of death. So far removed was he from even the concept of well-being that I could not imagine what he had looked like as a healthy man.

Yet whenever Tyrone's eyes met his, even for fleeting seconds, Martin's eyes brightened in the most astounding way with affection, admiration, respect, gratitude, awe, and the most palpably tender love I had ever seen. The two touched frequently—pats on the shoulder, gentle hand clasps, Tyrone brushing Martin's thinned hair behind his ears or away from his forehead, Martin reaching out and resting his bony palm on Tyrone's forearm, thigh, or shoulder. Tyrone was devoted and dedicated to Martin in so classic and even saintly a way that I felt privileged to be present at so private and poignant a time in their lives.

Because Martin was so weakened, Tyrone answered most of my questions. Among the first was my standard inquiry into the history of their relationship, and I was extremely surprised at the opening answers: that Tyrone and Martin had met and become lovers only two years before. It was a startling piece of information. I knew that the nurse had been seeing Martin for three years. That meant, obviously, that the men had become lovers long after Martin had been diagnosed.

Naturally, I began to wonder why Tyrone had chosen to love this doomed man, especially at such mortal risk. That curiosity required that I learn as much as possible about Tyrone first. He was very open, and as he talked, I could not help but notice Martin's rapt and admiring attentiveness.

Tyrone was an only child, born and raised in Utah. When, in his early twenties, he revealed to his family that he was a homosexual, they rejected him outright: no debate, no hesitancy, no compassion, no attempt at understanding. In their eyes he was the lowest form of life, and they said so. They cut him off, and would not speak to him or even about him.

Tyrone had responded by rejecting his family. He left home and moved to San Francisco. There, surrounded by a supportive community of other gays, many of whom had moved to San Francisco for exactly the same reasons, he formed new, concentric circles of friends and surrogate family members, and declined even to send the most innocuous messages to his family in Utah—not Christmas greetings, not even a birthday card.

Several years before Martin and Tyrone met, Tyrone's mother had become grievously ill, sick enough to make her have second thoughts about her behavior toward her only child. She called Tyrone and made what he thought was a feeble—but what was in all probability heroic—attempt to reacquaint herself and reconcile their differences.

"I did not handle that very well," Tyrone said, as Martin watched in deepest sympathy. "Maybe she caught me off guard, but at the time I simply could not bring myself to forgive her. I was quite cruel in my rejection, and abrupt. I think I was even impolite. Petulant. I even hung up on her. Jesus," Tyrone sighed, "three months later, I received a letter from a cousin of mine, who basically chided me, *condemned* me, really, for not showing up at her funeral the month before. It was the first I had heard of it. To this day, that was *all* I had heard of it. She was dead and buried a month before I knew anything about it."

Tyrone's eyes glistened as he spoke, and Martin's gaze was locked on him. Then Martin's face seemed to relax into a strangely knowing gaze, his expression half spousal, half parental. As Tyrone struggled to tell of his mother's death, I struggled myself to avoid crying with him.

Suddenly Tyrone looked at me directly and said, "Then I met Martin." He paused to look at Martin, who was grinning peacefully. Tyrone continued, saying that since they had met, his whole source of happiness had been his relationship with Martin.

Perfect.

I looked over at Martin, too, and for a split second I suspected that he knew what I was thinking: that their relationship had given Tyrone the opportunity to dedicate himself to a loved one in the way that he had not dedicated himself to his mother. This painful and tragic relationship was as much a gift to guilt-burdened Tyrone as it was to stricken Martin. I was continuing to work this out in my mind as Tyrone continued to speak rhapsodically about their relationship, until he abruptly lapsed into a pause that filled the room with silence.

I looked up and saw the two of them gazing into each other's eyes. I tried to say how moved I was by their relationship, which I described as perfect in its unselfishness and the profound opportunities it offered, each to the other. Not only had Tyrone offered solace, comfort, and affection to Martin at a cruel and crucial time in his life, but Martin had given Tyrone a profound gift as well—the opportunity to repair his past, to care for an ailing loved one in the way that he had missed caring for his mother.

As I talked—probably droned—on about Tyrone's devotion and attentiveness allowing him to make up for what he could not do and felt he should have done, I noticed Tyrone crying and nodding his head in agreement, while Martin smiled knowingly, even happily, as if I were saying words that he had only been waiting to hear.

As if that weren't sufficiently moving, Martin then looked directly at Tyrone and said the rest of what I was thinking:

''I've been waiting for this moment.''

Tyrone nodded. He knew it now, too.

''I've been waiting for you to understand,'' said Martin, ''that not only have you given me the gift of love, but that you've paid your penance. I've been waiting for you to let go.''

They embraced, weeping. I embraced the two of them, also weeping. I don't recall a more profound or touching moment in my life. The irony loomed as if it were a fourth person in the room.

Martin was now free to die. He had somehow stayed his sentence, sidestepped the ''death cocktail,'' until he was sure that the person closest to him was free. Was it possible? We came to work every Monday morning, and the first item on the agenda was a reading of the list of AIDS patients who had died during the weekend. The list was shortest just before Christmas and New Year's, and longest just after the holidays. I had no doubts that people kept themselves alive for that last celebration of generosity, hope, and love. I have no doubt that Martin kept himself alive for the same motivations.

Martin died the following evening. Tyrone called days later to say that Martin had left me something and that he would drop it off at my apartment. I couldn't imagine what it was, but when Tyrone brought it to me, he presented the package with a wry, conspiratorial grin.

It was Martin's word processor.

It reminded me of my feeling about therapy as art. The artist sees and depicts what we know about ourselves and our world but have not yet developed the skills to depict for ourselves—to reassure and fortify ourselves in the face of doubt. It was my privilege on that San Francisco day to articulate what Martin Miller most assuredly knew about his life but lacked the detachment to envision and then sculpt into a communicable form. On another day and with another couple, I used improvised drama to reframe a perspective and reveal the perfection of a relationship. On this day I had used words, had processed Martin and Tyrone's relationship and given it back to them in simple prose, the art form that happened coincidentally to be their favorite and their livelihood.

POSTSCRIPT

Despite Tyrone Weeks's geographical and emotional exile from his family, who condemned his homosexuality and rejected him outright, he was driven, as we all are, to repair his damaged relationships with them, particularly with his mother. I believe that this drive was so strong that he was willing to imperil his emotional stability and even his life in order to achieve the balance he sought. He could not repair his relationship with his mother while she was alive, but the desire remained so powerful after she died that it even influenced his selection of a mate. In the interest of repaying that debt, Tyrone coupled with someone whom he knew he would have to bury. In fact, he may have coupled with Martin in part *because* he would have to bury him.

The power of deceased family members cannot be underestimated. We often inherit a legacy that for many of us, guides, and in the more extreme cases, even controls our lives. We often see in lesser forms how the powerful influence of tradition and the desire to repair our pasts manifest themselves in our choice of a mate.

It could be argued that there was no real problem with Tyrone and Martin or their relationship. Neither partner was acting symptomatically. Martin's choice to commit suicide was certainly understandable, and in that milieu, it was acceptable. I even find it understandable that his physiology did not cooperate with his willed attempt to die: The two lovers had a loose end that needed tying before they could part, as the nurse who referred them to me had suggested.

Out of pure generosity, concern, care, or altruism, Martin wished to communicate to Tyrone that Tyrone had paid his penance and made restitution for his past by devoting himself to Martin, and that Tyrone need not suffer anymore for his ruptured relationship with his deceased mother. And Tyrone wanted to hear this, especially from a person he loved and had cared for until death.

Ironically, neither of the two professional communicators was in a position to put the message into words. So I did. It was a privilege.

Posthumously, Martin described my simple contribution to their relationship by the gift he bequeathed to me—the word processor.

DOUBLE CROSS

New York, January 1986

Andy Himmel and Phyllis Abrams had lived together for six years, and although they were considering marriage more seriously than ever before, they were concerned simultaneously about the future of their relationship. Initially, they told their therapist, Pat, that they feared they were becoming bored with each other. They agreed that each was feeling neither thrilled nor inspired by the other. They had become completely familiar with each other's stories. Habits of Andy's that Phyllis had once considered endearing were now getting on her nerves. The details of managing everyday life together had become blandly routine, and neither partner was introducing any originality into the relationship. Or so they said. They worried therefore—and understandably—that formalizing their relationship might only accelerate its deterioration.

In the first half of their first session, they talked about the various ways in which a couple might become bored with each other. Their narrative, frankly, was boring. Andy was a set designer who worked at home. Phyllis was an administrative vice president of a computer software company; she worked in an office.

According to my notes, I was not present for the first two or three sessions with them because their troubles appeared to be fairly standard for couples of their age and station. I had assigned a therapist completing her post-graduate training at the Family Institute to their case. The therapist was to work alone and consult with me after the session, or each session, depending on how long she saw fit to work with the couple. I would not intervene unless the case required it, and this one did not appear to.

However, matters that at first had seemed simple and ordinary soon revealed themselves to be quite complex and extraordinary.

At some point in that first conversation, Andy revealed to Pat that before he and Phyllis shared their lives together, he had been a drug user—a drug abuser, for that matter, as he admitted after Pat probed the subject a little. He finally admitted that he had been a burned-out drug addict who had been remanded to a well-known, full-time, live-in, rehabilitation facility.

Slightly surprised at the revelation, partly because of how severe he had allowed the situation to become, Pat asked Phyllis if she had known this about Andy's past. Phyllis knew. She knew even more. As if in a card game, Phyllis saw Pat's surprise as a bid and upped the ante. Not only had Andy been *in* a treatment facility, Phyllis added almost casually, he had been asked to *leave.*

"Why?" Pat inquired, knowing that residential drug-rehabilitation centers were hard to get into and very hard to get out of. People tried to escape from rehab centers; they didn't ordinarily get expelled. "Why did they ask you to leave?" she repeated.

The couple immediately began evading the question, almost conspiratorially. They hesitated, exchanged knowing glances, and then skirted the subject entirely. Andy said, "Well, I have something of a temper . . ." and trailed off. Phyllis nodded, shrugged, and then looked down at the floor. Andy talked about his more distant past as a juvenile delinquent—a rebel, a free spirit, a creative person in an unappreciative world—then he returned for a while to the subject of marriage and his relationship with Phyllis. Respecting their reluctance to reveal what made officials expel Andy, Pat returned with him to the subject of the marriage and the relationship and asked if either of them could pinpoint a time, place, or incident where the decline might have begun.

Andy started to offer one possible answer when Phyllis interrupted to say that for a short time she had thought he was unfaithful to her. "I became suspicious for a while," she said, "but as it turned out, he wasn't. He wasn't being unfaithful. So it sort of blew over. More or less."

"What made you suspicious in the first place?" Pat asked.

Phyllis gave Andy a quick glance first, then said: "The clothes. The clothes in his closet."

"The clothes?" Pat asked, baffled.

"Yes. Women's clothes."

"She thought they were somebody else's," Andy explained. "That's obviously what made her think I was being unfaithful. I'm home all day. There are women's clothes in the closet; therefore, there must be another woman. But there wasn't."

"What were the clothes doing there?" Pat asked.

"They were mine," Andy answered. "They still are mine. I, uh, wear them sometimes. I dress up."

"That was also why the drug rehab people asked him to leave," Phyllis added.

"I didn't have my own . . ."

"He was stealing the girls' clothes and dressing up in them."

Pat's notes indicate that at that point, as the session ended, she sensed strongly that she might need assistance from other members of the team. The narrative had taken more turns than she felt her compass could completely handle, and she was feeling very vulnerable, close to overwhelmed, by the couple's evidently bizarre revelation. My notes indicate that I asked her to conduct one more session by herself, not so much because we didn't agree with her but because it was a very busy time. We had many cases to discuss, and we all were struggling with heavy schedules.

In the second session, having thought about it for a week, Pat asked Andy to tell more about himself. Despite their original complaint, boredom was not the problem. Pat was on her way to establishing Andy's cross-dressing as the problem in the relationship. He reinforced her initial judgment by revealing that he had been in psychoanalysis for the past seven years. She asked him about the focus of his psychoanalysis, and he admitted to her that it was his cross-dressing. He and his analyst had explored ways of making himself stop, but unsuccessfully thus far. Worse, the impulse to cross-dress seemed to be increasing of late, and he was worried about it, too. Whereas he normally would cross-dress during the week only, when Phyllis was not at home, he was starting to dress up on weekends, too.

"Before, you were doing this somewhat secretively, and now you're doing it right in front of her?" Pat asked. Andy nodded affirmatively.

"It's a little unsettling," Phyllis said, "a little frightening."

"Does it have any effect on your view of him sexually?" Pat asked.

Phyllis thought about the question and surprised Pat with her answer. "Not really," she said. "We have an unusually exciting sex life, at least in my opinion. We both have backgrounds in amateur theater, Andy more so than I, and he is an absolute master of acting out fantasies. He creates situations and plays them out, and if I share his imagination just a little bit and go along with the game, it's like becoming the character in a movie. Sometimes he creates characters in costume and sort of seduces me. It can be very exciting, but without risk. It's like having a hundred different lovers but the same love."

The session ended. Having clearly identified Andy as the patient, Pat found herself in the same position as Andy's psychoanalyst. During our meeting later that day, Pat asked

her supervisory team to observe the next session from behind the glass, because she no longer knew what to do. In
reviewing the videotapes, it seemed to me that Phyllis's last
remark implied tremendous complicity on her part. If fantasy and drama were so welcome a part of her life with
Andy, you wouldn't think his cross-dressing would be quite
as frightening as she said. I began to suspect, in fact, that
his accelerated cross-dressing might have some hidden purpose in their relationship. Pat agreed, and we said we would
watch the next session.

I don't think I heard the first ten minutes of that session,
my attention was so riveted on the two faces of Andy Himmel and Phyllis Abrams, whom I had never before seen.
Their resemblance to each other was so distracting, to my
mind, that it drowned out the sound of their conversation.

He actually was the prettier of the two, his features
slightly more delicate and his frame a bit smaller than hers.
He was even the more feminine-looking (though he was not
effeminate) in the sharpness of his nose and cheekbones.
Both wore their straight, thin, sandy blond hair cut short
with bangs. Both wore glasses—his wire-rimmed; hers plas-
tic but similarly unobtrusive. Pixie-like, they had hazel eyes
and the rosebud lips of children. They were roughly the
same height, though she looked taller when seated.

The similarity was eerie enough to draw me into the room.
I was aware of the information I had heard about these people, but I was also aware that the combination of that
knowledge and their physical similarity had caused some
tiny explosion in my mind, some hint of discovery, although I had as yet no fix on it. I knew only that I wanted
to know more about this woman who lived with this man
who cross-dressed and who already looked just like her. Pat
had made him the identified patient, but my overwhelming
interest was her. I asked her to tell us about her family background.

"Well, I have a sister," she said, as if responding directly to the stimulus for my curiosity. As a bonus she added: "My sister and I are twins."

Pat and I looked at each other. The direction of the therapy made an abrupt about-face.

Phyllis went on to describe her relationship with her sister and, mainly, their father, who insisted that they dress alike, though Phyllis always felt herself to be the chunkier, less well-behaved, and more unattractive twin. Sharon, her sister, always could control the father better than Phyllis could, primarily through coquettishness. She would become flirtatiously persuasive and cajoling to get whatever concessions she wanted from him.

Phyllis fluctuated between awe and envy when this happened, but she recalled spending more time admiring her sister's talents and abilities than feeling jealous of them. Phyllis even had made some sacrifices to allow her sister to leave home and fulfill both their wishes to attend a private college. Their father had made clear to them that they both could go away to school, provided that one chose a school within the state university system. He could not afford room, board, and tuition for two in private colleges. Knowing how desperately Sharon wanted to attend Skidmore College in Saratoga, New York, and how impossible it was for both of them to go there, Phyllis fibbed and said that she was uncomfortable about leaving home so soon after high school. Instead she devised a compromise plan that her father could afford. While Sharon enrolled at Skidmore, Phyllis would attend a community college for two years as a commuting student, and then finish her undergraduate work at a more distant state university college.

"Where is Sharon now?" I asked. "How is she?"

"She's fine," Phyllis said. "In fact, she's getting married soon. Too soon, as far as I'm concerned."

"You don't think she's ready for marriage?"

"Oh, no! Christ, she's ready. She's thirty-four! No. She's ready. It's me! I don't think I'm ready for her to get married. I've been on edge about it. I'm also a little anxious about going to a traditional, catered wedding—as a brides-maid, no less, at my age. It feels so prom-like, so high school. She's doing the whole nine yards, with the wedding gown and the bridal shower and the schlepping and the cocktail hour, throwing the stupid bouquet, all of that. Yuk!

"And also she's my sister. I mean, you understand that. She's getting married and moving to some suburb in New Jersey. My sister, who I grew up with and slept with and who was my closest friend, who knew what I was thinking most of the time . . . all of that. She's getting married to this very nice guy, who is nonetheless taking her to Jersey someplace. So it's just an uncomfortable stage for me at the moment. I'm a little uneasy about it. I think that's normal, don't you?"

Without hesitating, I made an intervention. I said that not only did I think it was normal, I thought it lent great logic to her relationship with Andy. I told her I often found it remarkable that couples with unique needs found each other and so exquisitely satisfied those needs. "Andy looks so much like you," I ventured, "I would imagine that when he's dressed, he looks exactly like your sister. For that moment he allows you to continue to have that wonderful relationship with your sister, even though she is no longer with you."

As obvious as that now seemed to Pat and me, Andy and Phyllis seemed stunned by the observation. One of the rewards of my therapeutic approach is getting to tell people that they are all right when they have been convinced that they are not. It's even more rewarding when the information comes as a shock, with recognition and acceptance yet to follow.

"I'm also not surprised," I continued, "that Andy is cross-dressing more at this moment than ever before, and is doing it so boldly in front of you. Somehow you must have communicated recently your heightened anxiety about truly separating from your sister now that her wedding is imminent. At your more or less secret request, Andy is replacing her for you, making a very suitable accommodation. While cross-dressing could be perceived as an act of selfish indulgence in many circumstances, here it appears to be one of devotion, loyalty, and protection." We ended the session with both of them dazed by the possibility that they may have been each other's best life discovery.

The next time we gathered, Andy talked about his psychoanalysis and about his various attempts to give up his cross-dressing. I asked how he went about it, what his ritual was. He told how he would awaken early in the morning and know by the way he felt that he was going to dress up that day. It would be inevitable. If he wasn't dressing in Phyllis's presence, he would wait eagerly for her to leave for work. As soon as the apartment was quiet, he would bathe, instead of taking a shower, using scented soaps and applying body lotion afterward. Sometimes he dressed layer upon layer, as sensuously as a stripper in reverse, in front of a full-length mirror, watching the transformation as if he were an actor. Other times he would dry his hair and apply makeup while still wearing his robe, put on undergarments first, and then dress more briskly and deliberately in front of the mirror, as if he actually were a woman and not transforming at all. Following that, he would take a walk, window shop, and enjoy his disguise; or, on the occasions that he hated that he was dressing again and felt guilty about it, he would take in a pornographic movie or even visit a peep show, always aware of the surprised glances of the citizenry as his pretty female character slipped into the forbidden shadows. Some patrons inside were fairly disgusting to him, and he hoped that the association would make him see his own behavior as similar and thus be better able to stop it.

When I heard that—and it was the second time I had heard about his efforts to stop—I challenged his previous therapy. I said I thought it a mistake to change something that evidently was so much a part of him, a function of his creativity and individuality in general, his background in the theater more specifically. What harm did he perpetrate in testing the limits of his imagination? In some ways, I said, his ability really had been in the service and to the benefit of his relationship with Phyllis. It allowed him to be an extraordinarily creative lover, as she had described him. It also gave him a marvelously imaginative tool for helping her maintain her integrity as a twin sister. He could refashion himself as her twin. "Who else on earth could have done that for her?" I asked him. "What a gift!

"Maybe what really troubles you is the feeling that you have little or no control over your cross-dressing," I said. "What if you were to honor this inclination of yours, this creative ability? Perhaps then you would wrest control of it. Let me make a prescription for you. Instead of leaving this activity to the whim of spontaneity, I want you to make it a scheduled ritual. Institutionalize it. Choose the day that you are going to dress and then enjoy its stages. Indulge it. Take your bath, put on your makeup and your undergarments, watch yourself become an attractive woman, and applaud your talent for it."

"Yes!" Andy exclaimed, as if he understood absolutely. "But I won't do it on weekends."

"See? You're already taking control of it," I said, as our time ran out.

The next time we saw them, not enough time had passed for Andy to have tested the effects of the prescription, though he did tell us that he had not cross-dressed on the weekend. Neither he nor Phyllis seemed as upset or frightened as they had been, but all the indications were inconclusive. We decided to let a few more weeks pass before we saw one another again. When we did, two weeks later, Phyllis was visibly depressed. Her face was drawn and colorless; she seemed to have dressed haphazardly, at least for a working executive woman in New York, and we asked right away if she was feeling all right. She said she was depressed but that she could not answer why. We asked Andy if he could offer any explanation for her depression, and he wisely offered one that turned out to make perfect sense. He said that he was not sure, but that he had been considering the possibility that his refraining from cross-dressing in front of her might have precipitated her depression. "I've taken more control of it," he said, "and it seems to have made me a little bored with it. So I haven't been doing it at all, and the change, in the absence of any other change, seems to be what has affected her."

"I'm not surprised," I said. "Let's look at it. If you were cross-dressing less, then Phyllis might be missing her sister more and feeling depressed about the separation that is looming in her life. You probably have been protecting her from the inevitable depression she would feel about the separating. So her depression now is both understandable and positive. She *must* feel bad about her sister; it's natural and necessary. You protected her as much as you could have, and maybe more than you should have."

"I should tell you, then," Andy said, "that we've decided to get married after all. We're sort of engaged. I proposed."

"That's wonderful," I said. "And look how you've changed your relationship! She was losing a sister; you were protecting her from feeling bad about the loss, in effect by replacing her sister. But now you've stopped doing that and offered another form of love and protection, a more conventional form."

During the next few sessions, Phyllis continued to be depressed, and Andy did not cross-dress. He indulged himself only once in five weeks. Phyllis protested repeatedly that she was concerned about her depression, and I responded repeatedly by saying that she should not worry. I told her, first, that she *should* feel depressed, that anyone in her circumstances had a right to depression; and second, that she should not worry about feeling too depressed because if she descended too far, Andy would dress up and cure her of her depression.

Sometime around the seventh or eighth session, Phyllis confessed that she had been unable to sleep. She had insomnia. She added, however, that she had suffered insomnia as a child, so she was familiar with it, more or less. Then she added that as a child, she had suffered from depression, too, mainly because her sister was so successful.

I said that the depression and the insomnia did not surprise me, either, and in saying so, I think I surprised her again. I told her that she merely was suffering whatever she had suffered as a child. She had postponed this inevitable separation so successfully for so long that she had to go back to her childhood maladies to ache for it. "You're finally missing your sister," I said, "and you are having the same reactions and feeling the same feelings you felt the first time you were threatened with exactly this separation.

"All these seem to me to be part of your attachment to your sister," I said. "They all are reproductions of past emotions, reconstructions of past behavior in past relationships. You were the depressed twin as a child. You were an insomniac, which focused your parents' doting, parental attention on you and freed Sharon to become independent, gave her the freedom to go off and be herself. These things were part of a system of sacrificing yourself to allow Sharon to break away. She finished becoming independent, but maybe you did not. It seems to me that what you never accomplished was separating yourself from your sister. She is forcing that upon you now by getting married, and thus fully embracing her own independence.

"It also seems to me that this is precisely the right moment in your life for you to accomplish that unfinished part of your past. Your sister is getting married; your fiancé, Andy, is changing, and he has invited you to change your relationship together, and you seem to be ready to make the move. I would like to suggest that from now on, you try to make the best use of your insomnia. When you are awake, suffering this problem from your past, use every moment of that time to think about ways of developing your independence. That should include taking control of how close and how distant you want to be with your future husband, by asking him to be close or distant. So far you have been communicating by some secret method, and he has been picking up the messages, but I would like you to take more direct control over telling him what you want and need.''

The next two sessions were routine follow-ups. Their progress seemed slow, but it was progress. Phyllis said that she had been following the prescription. She had been asking Andy to cuddle her more, for instance; she also had been spending more time doing tasks alone that she enjoyed doing by herself. She mentioned more or less matter-of-factly that she had been sleeping better, too.

Midway through the tenth session, which turned out to be their last, Phyllis, seeming very relaxed, slipped into a discussion about their wedding plans and mentioned casually how frustrated she was feeling about her father's insistence that she and Andy have the same kind of wedding as Sharon—a traditional, catered affair with tuxedo-clad ushers, identically dressed bridesmaids, and all the accoutrements that Phyllis associated with barely post-adolescent unions. Both Phyllis and Andy were looking healthy and happy by this time; she was sleeping regularly, and each said he or she felt more in control of their own lives as well as their relationship. Suddenly I hit upon an idea that I thought could help punctuate the end of their therapy and begin the next chapter of their lives. I told Phyllis to approach her father and tell him precisely the kind of wedding that she wanted.

''But tell him,'' I said, ''just the way you would imagine Sharon telling him. Use her methods of convincing him and winning him over. Be coquettish, if that's what she would do. Be as flirtatious as she would be. Win him over exactly the way your sister would.''

She looked at me, smiling almost sagely, but waiting for more, for a kicker or a wrap-up line.

And one came to me.

"That way," I added, "you will become your own twin."
Her smile broadened.

POSTSCRIPT

Typically, we underestimate the powerful influence that siblings have over one another. Traditional psychology places a tremendous emphasis on the parent-child relationship, but we grow up with our brothers and sisters, and they influence us almost as profoundly as do our parents. In those relationships we learn about competition, friendship, sharing, protectiveness, and trust.

The "Double Cross" case illustrates the idea that our relationship with a sibling may be even more powerful than one with a parent. Here, a woman's conflict over separating from her twin sister becomes the pivotal issue in her relationship with a man—in fact, a mate. Metaphorically, and unwittingly, the couple tries to solve the woman's conflict by coming together, so to speak, in a re-creation of the relationship that the woman fears is about to change. They view Andy's cross-dressing a problem because they have not examined it from the perspective that it either solves a problem or postpones Phyllis's having to face one. While cross-dressing happens to be in Andy's repertoire (treated in his previous psychoanalytic therapy as a sexual deviation resulting from his improperly passing through the oedipal conflict), the extreme and exaggerated role it plays at this juncture in his relationship with Phyllis clearly identifies it as a problem-solving metaphor: it both protects Phyllis and gives her time to deal with her problem.

How did I see this so quickly when the first therapist, Pat, did not? To begin with, I entered the room already armed with the information the couple had so slowly and hesitantly offered Pat. I knew that I was about to confront a couple who were anxious and upset about the man's growing compulsion to cross-dress in the presence of the woman he purported to love. With that in mind, I was struck instantly by their physical resemblance, as I now am sure Phyllis was struck the very first time she laid eyes on Andy. The first element of her attraction to him may well have been his resemblance to her sister.

Secondly, I think that, consciously or otherwise, she detected my recognition and was sufficiently relieved by it to reveal immediately that she had a twin sister—a statement that appeared to emerge completely free of any context but obviously did not. She saw that I saw that Andy looked just like her, and then she rushed almost eagerly to explain the resemblance. Thus, after the first few minutes of our encounter, it made perfect sense to me that she was a twin; and it made good sense that when Andy dressed as a woman, he probably looked like her sister. It did not take Phyllis very long to reveal, still without realizing it, what generous and positive function Andy's seemingly aberrant behavior might have served: specifically, easing the pain of anticipated sibling separation. Generally speaking, people who care about each other ache to be able to smooth the partner's way or ease his suffering.

While Andy and Phyllis said they were eager to eliminate the disturbing symptom from their lives, I was concerned that the separation of the sisters would take time and that altering Andy's cross-dressing too rapidly might cause even more havoc. Because his accelerated cross-dressing stemmed from a motive outside of their consciousness, they were not in control of it—not as much as they could be. My idea, then, was to help them ritualize the phenomenon, to bring it into their consciousness and master the ritual of it so they could decide how to use it and when to give it up.

One of the main tactical ingredients in this case, as in many of the others, was to recognize that society at large would pass negative judgment on Andy for his actions. He already had been judged in previous therapy as being defective, which to me made Andy's bold resumption of the activity all the more generous and self-sacrificial a gesture. Once we identified his resumption of cross-dressing as a noble and creative, protective activity, and not necessarily a symptom of sexual deviation, he was free to exercise control over it. Once he had control, he could choose to employ it to rescue Phyllis when he saw that she couldn't endure her very natural anguish, or not to rescue her when she seemed able to endure it. Thus do many patients who have already invented a marvelously creative process for solving their problems solve them more efficiently once they recognize the course they have chosen and receive some encouragement for it.

By encouraging Phyllis to incorporate the opposite and complementary traits of her sister, I was encouraging the continuation of the process of sibling identification that would allow Phyllis metaphorically to take from her sister what she envied—and to complete the twinship in her sister's absence.

JINGLE JANGLE

New York, 1985

THE MANLEYS HAD BEEN MARRIED FOR ALMOST A DECADE, AND now that both were approaching their fiftieth birthdays, they found themselves with a four-year-old son and a seemingly impossible, mutually destructive relationship. Arthur Manley was out of work; Agnes was back *to* work. Arthur took care of the child and demanded that Agnes recognize that contribution; she recognized only his loutishness and berated him constantly for his inability to find a job.

They were a Broadway couple, characters from a 1930s James Cagney movie, catapulted by time warp into the television age. She wrote would-be pop and show tunes and earned a steady income by composing jingles for a third-rate advertising agency. He was an accomplished stage actor, an early graduate of the Actor's Studio, a Geoffrey Chaucer scholar, and a musical classicist.

I learned all that within ten minutes of our first session, most of it from Agnes, who punctuated her pronouncements with almost a dancer's extension, dramatic and grand.

"The man will not work!" she said, thrusting her palms forward in theatrical exasperation. *"That's* the problem! He will tell you that I am a shrew, that I criticize him constantly, that I give him no slack, that I interrogate him about his fruitless interviews and his elaborate telephone canvassing to old, washed-up cronies and vague new acquaintances; and when I uncover the fruitlessness or expose his telephone wanderings as no more than masturbatory, that then I mock him, humiliate him mercilessly, criticize him incessantly. And do I? Yes, I suppose I do. Why? Because it drives me insane that he wastes himself so and then lies about it, both to me and to himself. He says he tries to get jobs, but when you examine it, he doesn't really try. Not a whit. He dooms himself from the start, I think because he's become very comfortable doing nothing, being supported. Well, I am not comfortable with it. I resent it bitterly, and I won't have it. Things are going to have to change!"

Her performance ended, I turned to Arthur. A large man with huge shoulders and a completely bald head, he spoke with a deep, resonant voice, heralded, it seemed, by slow, sweeping hand gestures, forefingers pinched against his thumbs, as if each hand were wielding a baton. "It is true," he said in a voice that reminded me of James Earl Jones, "currently I have no role to play except at home, and Agnes has no patience with that, as she has exhibited little or no patience in recent months with other of my characteristics. I find that to be particularly ungrateful, as I have shown her nothing so much as patience during the nine and a half years we've been together, through some very difficult times and issues."

"Of course," Agnes interrupted quickly. "I am a recovering alcoholic; also a recovering compulsive spender, a credit card abuser, though I have not indulged in these delicacies in a couple of years. In either."

"There was a time," said Arthur, "and sometimes it seems as if in Agnes's mind it was long, long ago and far, far away, when she was not gainfully employed, and moreover, when she simultaneously spent our earnings as if she were contributing to them, and then doubly. It was a trying time, as I am sure you can imagine, and we managed to struggle through it, she with the help of Alcoholics Anonymous and I with the help of their tandem organization, Al-Anon. There were many disappointments; there was much frustration. . . ."

"What he is trying to tell you," Agnes said impatiently, "is that when my compulsive drinking and spending was the problem in our marriage, he served heroically as the patient and uncritical life partner who silently suffered while cooperating valiantly in my rescue from the abyss; and that now, when his compulsive sloth is threatening to snap our twig, I, the insufferable shrew, cannot summon equal saintliness to save the marriage." She threw her right hand away on the word *marriage*, and then allowed the same hand to fall limply back onto her lap with a dull whack of punctuation. There was a pause.

"She has been shrew-like," Arthur said.

"Are you a shrew?" I asked.

"I have been shrew-like," Agnes said. "I don't like it in myself when I hear the sounds escaping my mouth—they have an unflattering, acidic ring to them—but honesty dictates that I admit some complicity here. At times I've been quite awful. But it's just so infuriating to me, this inertia."

"Well, you are here, both of you," I said. "That's movement."

"Yes," she said. "The bottom line is this: Arthur will tell you that he feels I owe the marriage this last attempt, as if to reciprocate for whatever suffering he legitimately, I must say, endured through my personal crises, as well as on behalf of our son, Jonas, to whom Arthur is exceedingly close, and to whom, I must say also, he is quite a wonderful father." She paused again. "I have agreed with him—do agree with him—though for what reasons I am not exactly sure. I'm hoping that at bottom, they are the right reasons, that some genuine affection and respect and even love remains beneath my anger, although it has been festering for quite some time now. Even when I am feeling my worst, I know that I love our son, and I know Arthur loves our son, and I feel that something vague and primeval about that obliges us both to pursue the mending of this marriage, for a time at least.''

I asked Arthur if he had anything to add, and he shook his head. Agnes had accurately stated both his and her positions in the matter. He was satisfied with that, and I, encouraged. I told them that I wanted to see them separately next time.

Because of scheduling difficulties, I saw Agnes alone first. I asked her to tell me more specifically about Arthur's failed attempts to get a job. She did so with enthusiasm. She described how, after a series of elaborately defended postponements and nearly furtively conspired and then cancelled re-appointments, Arthur would make a ceremony of going to an audition for a part or an interview for some other theater-related position. She would worry about him all day and invariably find him that evening moping about the apartment, and she would know that he had failed to land the part or the job. She would then ask him for a blow-by-blow description of the meeting; he would comply; and when he got to the parts where he was supposed to be self-assertive and confident, she would interrupt his sad narrative and predict correctly whatever his response was to the interviewer's query.

"You told him that you did not have *that* much experience in musicals, right?" Agnes might say.

Right, he would answer, in his apparent shame and depression.

"You told her that you were reasonably confident that you could assist the casting director, though you never had worked in exactly that role before, right?" Agnes might say.

Right, he would agree.

Or, "Then," Agnes might pronounce, "you interrupted to say that although you had years of experience in the theater, the day-to-day nitty-gritty of daytime television acting was somewhat alien to you, right? But you thought that with a little time, you could master it eventually, right?"

Right again.

The predictability and the inevitability eventually would set Agnes off. She described her harangue to me with what seemed like rehearsed mastery:

"Why aren't you telling these people that you are brilliant?" she portrayed herself as demanding of him. "Or a genius, or more experienced than anyone they have ever met; or that you can bring to their silly, stupid job a wealth of talent and experience the likes of which no previous holder of the stupid job has ever brought? Why don't you tell these people those things? Why do you hang-dog, and mope, and equivocate, and hesitate, and self-destructively shrug yourself out of every goddamned encounter you have with such people?"

She would go on like that, she said, watching Arthur sinking lower and lower into his shame, until he evidently bottomed out and began to rise again in growing outrage at her hammering.

"I . . . have . . . my . . . pride!" he would answer slowly, teeth clenched, beginning to seethe openly.

"Pride in what?" she would snap. "In what you do? You don't do anything! When you finally get a job and do something, you may be able to regain your pride. Right now you have nothing to be proud of!"

Finally, Agnes said, Arthur would steam, huff, rise from his self-pity, stand, and erupt. She would realize for a second that she had gone too far again; she had been a shrew again, but it already would be too late.

"I have my honor to be proud of!" he would intone. "I have also my background, such accomplishments as I have documented over three decades; I have my mind, my study, my wit, and my skills. I have my standards, God damn you, beneath which are these jobs you so accurately describe as silly and stupid. And finally, I have my son, whom I love and care for, and whom I taxi to and from his preschool, and whom I teach and nurture, and whose frail and fragile and sensitive needs I secure as two parents might, were they both present and then so inclined."

Arthur would then storm out of the apartment and take a walk in the park, leaving Agnes behind to simmer, alternately enraged at him and at herself.

"It's amazing how you bring him out of his depression," I said to Agnes.

"What?"

"Well, at the end of the argument you just described, Arthur no longer was depressed."

"No, he was enraged."

"He also was asserting himself, as you had hoped he would."

"Well, yes, but to me."

"Of course to you. You are the one person with the sensitivity to see both his pain and his worth. I think you sense that he may be giving up on himself, or may already have given up on himself, or have given up on whatever dreams he once had. When he returns home with the evidence, depressed, you sense the depth and the origins of his depression and force him to fight his way back out of it. It's a very sensitive and generous act, because in order to do it, you have to become shrew-like, and you seem to find that terribly distasteful."

"I do," she said sadly. "It is terribly distasteful."

She thought for a moment. "I do perceive Arthur as having given up on himself, but I thought it was because of the way he wasn't doing anything about finding himself a job. It's more shocking to think that he might have given up entirely."

"So, then you behave in such a way that his mood changes from depression over his failure to sell himself to anger at your criticism, to self-righteousness and pride to justify his not taking an unworthy job, until he storms out of the house very much strengthened for the encounter. I just saw a production of *Man of La Mancha* again. On the one hand, you're like Sancho's character, helping Arthur tilt at windmills, because you believe in this man and in his dream. On the other hand, your heart tells you that he knows these are just windmills, because he attacks them so halfheartedly. Then, and therefore, he fails to have any effect. He is a man of many talents and passions who feels he has not succeeded in his career, although he certainly has succeeded in other ways—as a father, for instance. But the fact that he might have given up on his dream of making a contribution through theater—worries and concerns him, nearly defeats him, until you once again protect him from that. You force him to give himself hope and pride—''

Agnes had been silent. She interrupted, gazing off, ''It's really interesting. I can remember being out of control in my anger, and looking at him while I'm yelling, and having it go through my mind with such clarity that this is exactly what he wants.''

''Somehow he never gets *too* despairing over his failed job negotiations,'' I said.

''Right,'' she agreed. ''I give him a chance to feel superior, to say, 'I'm Arthur Manley, and I am worthy of better treatment than this!' ''

''He rises up from despair in an inflated way, and this mobilizes him and lifts him out of depression.''

''God, you're talking Al-Anon now. The enabler.''

''So how did you develop this talent?'' I asked. ''What was your family life like?''

She said, as if in the process of discovery, that her mother had been a shrew to her father, and that the behavior had had a very profound effect on her, now that she thought of it. She had vowed that she would never be like that; instead she would be a kind woman. Now, ironically, she found herself in the same position as her mother, responding to the same situation by being the same kind of wife. I asked what she meant by the ''same situation,'' and she answered that her father had frequently been out of work, too.

Now I had important additional information. Agnes not only was saving her husband, she was saving her memory of her mother. She had broken a promise to herself not to be like her mother, and in doing so had validated her mother's behavior. By responding to her similar history exactly as her mother had responded, she effectively understood and forgave her mother. I told her that. I said that in the same circumstances, she behaved the same way as her mother had, though she wanted to behave in a kinder way, which suggests the possibility that her mother might have wanted to be kinder, too; probably saw the ugliness of her behavior more clearly than she saw the necessity for it. I suggested to Agnes that she was being intensely loyal to her mother, breaking her vow to prove that her mother had not lived her life in vain. Further, she was in a way sacrificing herself, risking her own stability to stabilize her family, just as her mother might have done.

Having identified in their families of origin the circumstances that gave meaning to the presenting problem—their repeating marital argument—I sought a way to disrupt the argument. I chose a technique called "a reversal," first described by Murray Bowen, of Georgetown University, and later amplified by Peggy Papp. On the surface, the idea appears somewhere between painfully and comically simple. In effect, the therapist tells a patient troubled by, say, her own obsessive arguing, that she should stop arguing. Armed with the context of Agnes's hidden loyalties to both her mother and her husband at the expense of her own integrity, I would offer her an alternative loyalty, one with which she was intimately familiar. I assured her that I would be with her for the consequences. Then, I asked Agnes if she could behave in a fashion opposite from her pattern. "Be faithful to your vow to be kind," I said. "It's something you long to achieve, anyway. Can you do that? Can you break the pattern without telling Arthur what you are doing, if only to see what would happen?"

"Aha," she near whispered, adrift in thoughts of her mother. "Of course I can. Yes."

My session with Arthur was less dramatic, but no less revealing. He corroborated in the main what Agnes had said about his job interviews, her subsequent interrogations, and the eruptions that followed; but he added his interpretation of himself as a rock, as the stabilizing force in the family, always available to and supportive of his temperamental and ambitious wife. He repeated in detail how for the nearly ten years of Agnes's vodka and Visa card addictions, it was she who could not find work or who, having found it, could not complete a whole day of it without forfeiting the position. When she became what Arthur so carefully called a recovering alcoholic, she returned home with new matrices of anxieties, worrying about competing with the younger, slicker, even more ambitious women, fretting about managing to straddle the often conflicting roles of working woman and mother, let alone wife.

"In a dispute replete with irony," he said, "she criticizes me for the very solution my unemployment has provided to her most severe dilemma, that of leaving Jonas, perhaps all day, with a stranger, and thus suffering the standard anxiety over the choice of caretaker, as well as the additional guilt and anxiety that a woman so addicted to neuroses can heap upon herself. I believe that she relies on me to stay home even while she is screaming from her lectern that I should get out."

I asked him about his childhood. He answered that it had been nearly perfect. His father, who owned a seat on the New York Stock Exchange, made enough money so that nobody in the family ever had to worry about finances. His father's financial success freed his mother, he said at first, to stay home with her children, though she, Arthur was quick to point out, had established impressive credentials independent of her husband's accomplishments or expertise. His mother, certified as a teacher, had attended night school and earned her degree in law. Then, he said proudly, over her husband's traditionalist objections, she had passed the New York State bar exams and had been admitted.

"She never practiced, though," he said. "Like the heroine of a much more modern novel, she was a financially secure, potentially independent housewife and mother.''

''She sacrificed a career to stay at home with her children,'' I said. ''That sounds very much like what you are doing.''

''I beg your pardon?'' he intoned. ''I appreciate the complimentary suggestion, but I am currently a man with no career to sacrifice.''

''Yes, but look at the message you received from your very happy and very successful family: a happy and successful home is one in which one parent remains at home, and the other goes off to work to earn a living. You have your mother's dilemma, and you've only had it for four or five years. The price she paid for a happy family was her career. Whatever dreams she had had for career accomplishment—''

''It's too high a price,'' he said.

''I'm not saying you should pay it. But recognize your obedience to your mother's heroic lesson, which is one of tremendous sacrifice. In honor of that memory, your success as a father, in your mind, may depend to a great extent on your abdication of career goals.''

He shrugged, more or less.

I offered a companion reversal to my prescription for Agnes, this one tailored from the context of Arthur's repeating behavior.

''I have an idea to prescribe something for you,'' I said. ''I'd like you to try it for a while. Don't change anything about the way you live, but change the way you talk about it to Agnes. Whenever you are about to tell her of a job you think you cannot get or an interview you feel you've failed at, stop yourself and tell her instead about yourself, about how you feel, about what you enjoyed that day regarding your time with Jonas. Handle your career concerns by yourself for a while. Don't tell her about what you perceive as your failures. That might just be your way of reassuring her that you're going to be home with Jonas, the way you feel one of you ought to be.''

Arthur looked off to the left and nodded slowly but affirmatively.

I saw them for two more sessions, together. In the first, Agnes said that Arthur seemed much less depressed, had been out of the house more, seemed to be emerging from a self-entombing shell. He agreed, saying that it felt good, though he couldn't put his finger on exactly why. He added that his wife had been uncharacteristically kind and patient with him, *sweet* was a word he used several times. Both of them seemed uneasy. I mentioned that, and both agreed that they *were* sort of uneasy. The changes they perceived seemed delicate. I suggested that perhaps the patterns of their marriage were dying, and they were uncertain about what patterns might replace them. ''You, Arthur, have stopped confessing your failures, and you, Agnes, have stopped criticizing him for them.''

''I have also been considering a different kind of work,'' said Arthur. ''In fact, I may this week be accepting an offer for a position as director of a municipally subsidized community theater in Jersey. Most of the rehearsals and performances,'' he said, nodding to Agnes, who obviously was learning of this for the first time, ''take place in the evenings or on weekends.''

''Arthur!'' Agnes squealed.

''So, you can still be with Jonas in the afternoons,'' I said.

''Precisely. And get back into the . . . flow, I might call it.''

I told them that their therapy was ended and the rest up to them, but added that I would like to see them one more time, perhaps in a month. In that last session, they seemed happier, though still tentative, still a little worried. Arthur spoke proudly of his ensemble and their performance schedule; Agnes said that even Jonas seemed happier for the subtle changes in their lives.

The Manleys' dispute was an argument with a perfect

purpose. It had become stubbornly but quite usefully a part of their relationship, and it therefore had repeated itself and become enduring. Couples who deeply care about each other frequently behave this way. Usually, when they are repeating the same fight again and again, and they cannot seem to conjure up a new one, a very stubborn, critical cycle is going on. This particular argument lifted Arthur Manley out of his despair, allowed him to remain faithful to his family of origin by being the steady rock, the one who stayed home while the other worked outside the home; and simultaneously it allowed Agnes to be faithful to her family, despite her stated determination not to be faithful.

In both cases, their allegiance to their ideas of what was right was at the expense of their own pursuits. In both cases, their behavior was born of generosity, not venality. She gave up her vow, which basically was to betray the memory of her mother; and he gave up his career, in order *not* to betray the memory of his, making them an exquisite match for each other. The intervention respected both their willingness to help each other and the positive attributes of the behavior of their families. It also gave them opportunities to pursue their own needs, while still exercising their natural generosity and loyalty. Agnes could be kind; she had earned the right. Arthur found a way to follow his career interests without betraying his idea of nobility and heroism, of sacrificing career for family.

Early the next year, I read that Agnes had won an award for a jingle, and that Arthur had won regional acclaim as a playwright-producer-director, for producing and writing a play called *Live at 55*. Aware that some of the finest dramatic writing was autobiographical, I often wondered about the subject and wished I had seen the show.

POSTSCRIPT

Always, in dealing with a couple, particularly a married couple like the Manleys, the question lurking beneath any conflict is whether their union is going to be perpetuated, —whether it ought to be, whether they want it to be. However, I proceed as if the question of separation or divorce is irrelevant. I attempt to identify the way in which the couple's problem is maintaining the relationship and keeping them emotionally distant at the same time. Once we succeed in separating the couple from the problem, the couple better knows the reasons why they are together and whether or not they ought to be. In my experience, a couple should not think about separating from each other until they have separated themselves from their problem, and in so doing, have effectively solved it.

I followed a fairly well-defined clinical map in the Manley case, because the situation represented a quite common and even classic scenario in couple relationships, though this couple's was more poetic. From the personal unhappiness each partner expressed, I sensed that each was making a sacrifice to attain a certain stability—and that neither one was satisfied with such stability as had been achieved in the trade-off.

My charted course would lead me first to learn what I could about their respective pasts and then to find out how their problems serve both their histories and their present situation—and at what cost. Once I discover the dilemma, I can identify it to them and offer some suggestions for compromise or accommodation. A relatively unimpassioned experience for me, it is nonetheless exhilarating in an intellectual way, as I imagine sifting through a newly discovered site is for an archaeologist.

Common to every case is the stubbornness of a problem when the historical and the current elements merge. In this case it was more pronounced because both members of the relationship were acting out of loyalty to the traditions of their families of origin, but each was trying to rescue the other as well. With a massive rescue process going on, each was also sacrificing something important to himself. In this case, the dilemma was that the need to be faithful to their pasts conflicted both with their personal desires and with the desire to allow the other partner to be true to his own past—a triple conflict. Normally, there is a ready-made conflict between the desire to be loyal to one's own tradition while at the same time honoring one's partner's tradition. The Manleys threw in, as well, surrendering their personal ambitions in order to effect the rescue. The new solution had to let each member find a way to honor both his past and that of his partner while also achieving his personal ambition.

Although the Manleys' perception of their situation had changed, and some new behavior had emerged as a consequence, this new, more satisfying interaction was fragile at the time we recessed the therapy. But, because of the creativity and the drama they had employed to set up the original problem, I was confident that they would continue to expand positively on the new repertoire that was initiated in therapy. I was also confident that, given the positive experience we had together, they would return if they reached another impasse.

ACHIEVING
FAILURE

∎

What could be more relative than the notions of success or failure? We read newspaper accounts every year about retired professional athletes "failing" to gain election to their respective halls of fame, following decades wherein they achieved one herculean success after another. Olympians "fail" to win a gold medal, while winning a bronze instead. Exactly who is kidding whom here?

But in systems as intricate and beautiful as families, if we all adhere to reasonably measurable standards of behavior and accomplishment, we certainly can fail to achieve them, in which case I like to ask the question, "Well, what *did* we achieve, then?"

In this section, the longest, most complex story concerns a family that achieves multiple layers of however misdirected success directly as a result of the failure of their children to achieve conventional successes. In many families where one or more members fail to measure up to the family's standards, the failure itself is achieving a hidden goal: drawing attention away from a potentially cancerous disruption; serving as a diversion, to allow another family member to break into the light of success; permitting family members to remain loyal to the messages of their own pasts. So often, as in the story entitled "Holocaused," the failure is borne of generosity and self-sacrifice, and wholly within the failing family member's control, despite appearances to the contrary.

The paradox of failure is that you can succeed at it.

HOLOCAUSED

Sᴀʀᴀʜ Sᴛᴇɪɴᴍᴇᴛᴢ ᴡᴀѕ ɴɪɴᴇᴛᴇᴇɴ ʏᴇᴀʀѕ ᴏʟᴅ ᴀɴᴅ ᴀ ѕʏᴍᴘ-tomatic smorgasbord by 1982, when her family appeared at the Family Institute. Although Sarah's symptoms had shifted and changed over the years, she had been consistently agoraphobic for seven years and suffered severe and evidently physically painful anxiety over even the thought of leaving her house alone. She barely had finished high school through a home-study course tailored for her by an office of the New York City public school system, and she had made a few abortive attempts at work and college. At home, Sarah suffered severe, medically untraceable stomach pains and refused to be left home alone. Miriam, her mother, sometimes stayed in the room with Sarah at night and recently had taken a leave of absence from her supermarket job to remain at home with her sick child.

Sarah's eldest sibling, Ari, the eldest of Miriam's three children, was married by this time, living in Hartford and working as an accomplished family therapist. Dedicated as Ari was to helping her family, she had not succeeded in resolving any of the conflicts about Sarah; nor had any therapist or agency Ari recommended to them helped the family at all. Having read in her professional literature of a three-therapist team-treatment method (originated by three senior family therapists, Olga Silverstein, Peggy Papp, and myself), Ari had placed a desperate call to the Family Institute. The family then had agreed to treatment—to the joint sessions, to the videotaping, to the full participation the program required—in order to reassure Ari that they would make whatever sacrifices necessary to help Sarah overcome some of her obvious suffering and her consistent failure to recover or construct a life of her own.

It is unusual for a family with one so obviously symptomatic member to participate in family therapy. More often such families try to "get some therapy" for the troubled soul, as if a failing member of a family owes his fate to himself alone. The Steinmetz family was manifestly different. Not only were they tightly knitted, they were so well aware of the strength of this weave that family therapy seemed the only remaining logical approach even to them.

The program—requiring as it did the efforts and presence of three senior therapists during each therapeutic session, as well as in strategy meetings before and after each session—was reserved for the most difficult cases only. Intake material on the Steinmetzes did indicate that they had tried a number of therapeutic approaches and had been unsuccessful for years, and prior failure in therapy was a prerequisite for acceptance into our program; but Sarah Steinmetz's behavior in the very first session convinced all three of us that this case presented a serious challenge indeed.

The treatment team, consisting of Alice Tripp, Ruth Goldman, and myself, conducted at least four sessions devoted to learning the family stories and identifying the characters. During each, Sarah seated between her brother, Ira, and her father, Karl, alternately writhed, grimaced, moaned, grasped, and clutched in apparent agony at her father's and brother's hands, and then abruptly interrupted her anguish occasionally to sip, childishly, from a can of soda, as family members described their history, their feelings about her troubles, and how they dealt with them.

Sarah spoke in contradictory voices, sometimes with the

lazy, whiny squeak of a petulant little girl, sometimes with the labored, softened consonants and sloppily extended vowels of a drunk. She openly described herself as the center of the family, the problem around which everyone's lives pivoted. There was neither arrogance nor pride about her self-designation; it sounded more like a simple declaration of her role. She also declared herself incurable. "I'll always be like this," she said. "I know I'll never get better. I just have to learn to accept it."

Moreover, if you closed your eyes and listened to Sarah's moans—and we noticed this only when the video failed once during playback—they sounded weirdly orgasmic, intensifying and relaxing in waves, as the offending family member continued to elaborate or backed off.

Her face grew taut with pain, it seemed, at certain testimony more than others. She writhed when her mother mentioned the possibility of returning to work. She slapped her brother's hand punitively and snatched it back when he—handsome young man of twenty-six, who still lived at home and still was struggling to "find himself"—suggested he might someday want to be freed of her clutching.

Sarah's convulsive contractions could have interrupted all discourse—as they were meant to—but intertwined with world-changing events and involving characters from three generations, the following family history nonetheless emerged:

Miriam had been eight years old when German soldiers stripped her family of their land and all their possessions during the 1938 occupation of Austria. They seized Miriam's father and took him to Dachau, where he was imprisoned for years.

Torn between the anguish she felt over the loss of her husband and the terror she felt about the safety of her two daughters, Miriam's mother made a heart-wrenching decision during the weeks following the storm troopers' raid. She decided she would remain in Austria, for fear she otherwise might never see her husband again. Secretly she would send away her girls, Miriam and Fredda, to what she believed as the safety of Sweden, to live under the protection of sympathetic families there.

By the age of eight, then, Miriam felt desperately abandoned by her family. Though she lived safely in Sweden until 1946, she was separated from everyone, including her sister, who lived with another family in another Swedish city, too far away even for infrequent visitation.

Intellectually, Miriam always understood the logic of her mother's decision; it may well have saved her life. But emotionally, Miriam could not help but feel that, faced with the choice of staying by her husband or remaining with her children, her mother had chosen to be a wife first and a mother second. It was a hard slight to forgive, and Miriam never did.

By 1946, Miriam's parents managed to escape Austria and settled in Palestine. With the help of the Swedish government, Miriam and her sister also traveled to Palestine and were reunited with their parents. The family had barely had time to readjust, however, when sixteen-year-old Miriam was conscripted into the army, as the emerging nation struggled for its independence.

While serving in the army, Miriam met Karl Steinmetz. His family had fled Germany during Hitler's early rise to power. After a brief courtship, during which—consciously or otherwise—Miriam learned of a fundamental difference between her family and Karl's, Karl and Miriam married. Within a few years they had two of their three children, Ari and Ira.

In 1958, Miriam and Karl faced a dilemma not unlike that of Miriam's mother twenty years before. The parents of two children, they were living in a perilous place at a perilous time. Karl surely would be required to serve in the army again, and Miriam thus worried about her children growing up fatherless. However, leaving Israel to save her new family required Miriam's re-separating from the family the war

already had rendered near strangers. So before the Steinmetzes emigrated to the United States, Miriam extracted
from her parents a promise that they would follow in five
years.

Five years passed, during which time Karl's family did
emigrate to the United States. Miriam and Karl meanwhile
had a third child, Sarah. Miriam then received word from
her parents that her father's business commitments pre-
cluded his moving out of the country. He and Miriam's
mother would remain in Israel, they said. Crushed, feeling
once again abandoned by her family, Miriam formed an especially powerful bond with the infant Sarah.

Sarah responded tenfold.

In the early sessions of therapy we detected and discussed possible impediments to the process and tried to
overcome them by temporarily adding to the cast of characters, from whom we learned more than we expected, anyway. For instance, it occurred to us while reviewing the
videotapes that if we were to succeed in helping the family,
we would tacitly be declaring Ari a failure as therapist to
her own family. So we invited her husband, Marvin, to the
next session to redefine Ari as more separate, part of a different unit now, than the troubled family we hoped she
would turn over to us. However, we found out in that next
session that Ari was afraid to become less intensely connected to her parents' problems for fear she then would
expect greater emotional contact with Marvin, for fear that
Marvin ultimately would disappoint her the way she believed her father had disappointed her mother.

A subplot—a demanding-wife-vs.-withdrawing-husband
pattern—was beginning to emerge in two generations, at
least. We already knew that Miriam was disappointed in
Karl, also a supermarket employee, for his apathetic ambition, his marginal success as a provider; we knew that since
Karl's mother had died two years before, leaving Poppa to
Karl and Miriam's care, Miriam felt imprisoned by Karl's

family as well as abandoned by and estranged from her own.

We invited Karl's father, Poppa, to another session. Poppa declared *himself* the senior of the clan and accused his son of being "too lazy to change, too lazy to stand on his feet against his family."

"That's something I really don't like in him," Poppa said of the fifty-five-year-old Karl. "He gave too much over to his wife, and she is a demanding one. She is not only a demanding one; she is a commanding one!"

Ruth had been acting as the principal interviewer of the team, a deliberate choice based on her age and ethnicity. We had anticipated that this Holocaust-surviving family might believe, deep down, that their history made them different to the point of uniqueness, and that therapists consequently would never understand them. We hoped that by leading off with Ruth—Jewish and about sixty years old—we would implicitly counteract this kind of inherent roadblock.

Ruth asked Poppa how life had been with his wife. Poppa first answered that they had had a love affair for fifty years. Ruth pressed: "But you more or less followed your wife for fifty years, right? I mean, that's something Karl learned from you, how to be a devoted husband."

"I don't know," he answered in a thick German accent. "Because he is devoted, she got him so far that *she* is the man in the house. What I understood later on in my life was that the brain, or the nature, of a woman in feeling love is different from a man's feeling of love. A man can love one woman very much. The woman has no time for so much love, because she has children, she has her homework, and she has her part-time work, like the stitchery, which she likes very much."

"A woman loves her children more than she loves her husband. Is that what you're saying?" Ruth asked.

"Yes," he said, nodding briskly for punctuation. "You

see, for me, my wife came first in life. For her, the children
came first."

There we found a profound difference between Miriam's
parental family and Karl's. Somehow in the messages of
courtship, Miriam had discovered in Karl an honored family
tradition that demanded that, given the awful choice, a
woman always would stay with her children rather than her
husband.

From all of this, Ruth, Alice, and I constructed a hypoth-
esis describing the relationship between Sarah's symptoms—and to an extent, Ira's less obvious inability to tear
himself away from the family—and the family's various connections and disconnections: the children's failures were
functional.

In her children's failure to succeed outside the house, and
especially in Sarah's exaggerated inability to live without
Miriam always by her side, Miriam was protected from further familial separation. The conventional role of children
Ira's and Sarah's age was to leave home and become independent, or at least to be preparing to leave home. However, if Miriam's children were to make those moves toward
separating successfully, they would be abandoning their
mother, as they knew her own mother had abandoned her.

Also, they were members of a family whose paternal side
had a strong tradition of the mother–child relationship being more important than any other, and whose maternal
side held to a tradition of reading child–parent separation
as abandonment. Miriam felt tremendous pain for having
been abandoned by her mother as a child, as well as tremendous guilt for having left her mother behind as an adult.
The message to the children, particularly Sarah, was:
"Never leave your mother, and never allow her to leave
you." Karl was to support that. And fidelity to the message
required the children's failure.

Ira remained faithful to his mother by failing to become
independent and leave. Ari remained faithful by failing to
serve the family professionally and thus free her siblings to

leave. Sarah had transmogrified into a rock of fidelity, supporting her mother's needs almost single-handedly, by failing with theatrical heroism at life in general.

Olga Silverstein, Peggy Papp, and I had developed a strategy for helping families with such multi-layered dilemmas to reveal and define their choices. So Alice, Ruth, and I set about to use it, first persuading Ari to hand over her family to us without damaging herself in the process. We would debate the consequences of change for the family, while the family sat and listened to us. They would have to listen to their own dilemmas and choices being played out in front of them.

Our first debate would center around the possible consequences of Ari's turning them over to us. Each of us would argue from a pre-planned position. We had decided that Ruth, who was most identified with the parents by age and ethnicity, would surprise everyone by championing change, urging the children toward independence and therefore, she postulated, health.

Outrageous as it might have sounded to anyone who knew my normally positive view of change, I would represent the opposite view, the conservative approach, constantly suggesting that change would be costly to the stability of the family, that the current arrangement served everyone, that the risks of change would be too high (and the risks *were* high, especially to the fragile marriage of Miriam and Karl).

Alice would assume a third position—one of compromise, rounding out what we had determined were the family's dilemmas about change. In our debate we would voice and dramatize all of the elements we recognized that supported or negated change and its consequences. Alice would "see" the merit in both Ruth's exhortations and my trepidations, but she would be the advocate of marital happiness, and she would say that she believed that the family's problems could be worked out, whatever the risks involved. None of these debating stances were invalid; we could have changed places and argued with equal combinations of reason and passion for each. We were presenting the family with a more clearly defined version of their true dilemma. They could remain faithful to their family messages and stay the same, or they could change and risk the consequences.

I began.

I said I had some serious concerns about Ari turning the family over to us, because I thought that if we were to begin to help Sarah and Ira grow up, both marriages would be placed in jeopardy. "Without the constant problems of Ira and Sarah," I said, "the link between the women in the family might weaken, and you, Miriam, might turn to Karl and expect more of him. Then Ari might turn more to Marvin. And both you women might be disappointed. On that basis, I would recommend that for the time being, *you* two, Sarah and Ira, continue to have your problems. They provide a very important link for the women in the family, and they protect the two husbands."

Thus I planted the suggestion that Sarah and Ira were more in control of their failure than anyone might have imagined. I hoped that describing their unconscious motives as deliberate would force them to be conscious of their function. That, in turn, would place their failure under their control.

"Wait a minute!" said Ruth, picking up the debate but continuing to work within my control suggestion. "Whatever the consequences, Sarah and Ira have a right to grow up. I don't think that they should have to worry about their parents. Young people have to take care of themselves, not their parents."

Alice then addressed herself to the two married couples, saying, "I feel that it might stir up trouble in your marriages if Ari were to turn the family over to us for change, but I believe you can handle it. Miriam, it might be good if you did make more demands. It's important to concentrate on the issues between you and Karl, whatever they are. It might strengthen both marriages rather than hurt them. And I don't think the husbands need protection from that."

"Well, it's of no concern to the children at any rate," Ruth said. "They have to tend to their own business. However, let's leave the final decision up to the family, all right? We all agree there would be risks; we disagree on whether you should take them. You're the family; you decide."

The Steinmetzes showed up for the next session without Ari and Marvin. Watching them arrive, we determined that Ari's absence meant they had rejected my position in the debate, which held that Ari's remaining involved in therapy would be an open admission that neither marriage could withstand the consequences of change. We were on a way to a new challenge, the family effectively saying, "Go ahead, cure Sarah." Sarah, of course, continued to insist that she would never be cured.

While interviewing Sarah and Ira—the rest of us, therapists and family, watching from behind the glass—Ruth discovered a powerful alliance between them, in which they revealed that they cooperated to protect their parents, a form of loyalty pact we had seen before, especially in the families of Holocaust survivors. Ruth then tried to separate the two children over the issue of independence, cleverly suggesting that since Sarah practically had vowed by her protestations to remain ill forever and thereby provide her mother with a lifetime child, why shouldn't Ira leave the protecting entirely up to Sarah and move more comfortably toward his own independence? "Why should both of you take on this responsibility when one can handle it quite well?" Ruth asked boldly, once again asserting that Sarah reigned over her problems.

Sarah squeezed Ira's hand at this suggestion and writhed in a spasm of pain. But neither Sarah nor Ira protested Ruth's suggestion that their respective failures were serving to protect their parents. So the session ended with their troubles placed in a context new for them *and* for their parents, observing from behind the glass. Ruth's parting, incendiary, recommendation to Ira was to encourage Sarah to have more problems and free him from the responsibility a little.

The family had to carry Sarah up the stairs to the next session (though during it, she again interrupted her agonized writhing to sip Coke).

This session was devoted to an attempt to formally structure a new context for the whole family, one that viewed the children's failures as a means of protecting the parents. Having seen hints of that restructuring in the last session, everyone in the family seemed to know what was going on, and they were eager to evade, avoid, or deny it.

As if trying to show their doctors a miraculously healed wound in order to avoid more surgery, Karl and Miriam said that their lives had changed for the better in the intervening week. We had connected Sarah's symptoms to them and their marriage, and they were trying to disconnect them—and quickly. Miriam even had awakened Karl in the middle of the night to make love, an event so unusual as to suggest a total cure, thank you; so there really was no need to proceed further along the course we had only yet just begun. Miriam also had decided to return to work, she declared, as further evidence of a case closed, a job done, needs satisfied.

Sarah, however, had deteriorated, beginning the night they had returned home from therapy. We were not surprised. If Sarah was helping her mother avoid the marriage and choose her children instead, Miriam certainly would need a needy child to serve. Sarah's recovery would deprive her of that convenience.

Ruth began the session by asking Ira if he had done what she'd prescribed, encouraged Sarah to get worse, to fail, in effect, even more demonstrably. Ira equivocated, but finally said that he had not been in the house much that week. During the conversation Sarah moved from writhing and clutching to crying. Ruth, with laser-beam precision, addressed Sarah directly:

"Sarah, when you decided you were going to take this whole thing on yourself, did you decide about how far you were going to go with it? Or is this open-ended?"

Sarah leaned her head to the left, crying, but at the same time trying to hide or withhold a grin, which I took to be a smile of recognition, maybe even release. If our persistent suggestion had any merit at all, Sarah did have control over her failures. Sarah's smile revealed that she either suspected or knew that she did. Ruth continued, again questioning the logic of having both children fail to help the family when one failure would surely suffice.

As Sarah continued to writhe and cry, Ruth said to the rest of us, "You know, it's a very tough spot she's picked for herself. It's really one that we can empathize with. But, Ira, I suppose maybe it would help if you showed a little gratitude."

"Well," Ira said hesitantly as Sarah gripped his hand, "I don't think I've been entirely willing to do that, because I don't think I've been willing to let her take all that on. . . ."

"I was afraid of that," Ruth said.

"I predicted that," I said.

"I don't know what it is," said Ira. "I notice that now I'm getting angry. I feel like saying, 'Damn! Let go of my hand today!' But I have all these pictures in my head of what it's supposed to look like, if Sarah takes it all on. One is that she won't need to hold my hand anymore, and I'll be able to sit over here like this—"

"Nooo! Nooo!" Sarah whined, writhing in apparent pain.

"Sarah," I said softly but firmly, "I want to begin by complimenting you on your sound understanding for what happens in this family."

Sarah rocked, clutched her head, and whined, "I don't understand at all!"—but still with a slight trace of a smile.

"Well, let me explain what I mean. I think that you must have understood this week that your parents were getting closer, and that in fact they may even have started some love affair. In the most profound way you understood that, and you particularly understood the danger in that." Sarah looked at me, ostensibly perplexed. "What I mean is that if your mother continued to invite Karl to enter into a love affair with her, she would be choosing thereby to be a wife first and a mother second. And I think that you understand that she would feel enormous guilt about that. She might even worry that you and Ira might never forgive her, in the way she has not forgiven her own parents."

"You really bug me, Stanley!" Sarah cried. "I mean, some of the things you say! I am *not* out to save my family! I don't believe this!"

"Now, just listen to me a minute," Ruth interrupted. "You are caught in a very tight spot, and the dilemma is fairly clear to me that you are on the one hand really anxious to get on with your life, that you really want to leave. I think seeing Ira make some moves in that direction exaggerates that same desire of your own—to get a little freer, to live on your own, to do what you want to do with your life, to succeed. No? There is some of that drive, is there not? But, on the other hand, there is the other place—that were you to do that, you would be abandoning your mother." Sarah held her ears and shook her head.

The next session began with Ruth asking matter-of-factly, "Anything new since we last saw you?" and Sarah just as matter-of-factly answering, "I went to Boston for the weekend." It was very difficult, she said, but it was with that same childlike ambivalence that looks for approval in shocking the adult she is trying to please or impress—in this case me, the conservative one, because I "opposed" her breaking out and changing. The relationship with me was becoming beautifully dual, as if I were a demanding but loving grandparent. She wanted to rebel against me, but she wanted my approval, too.

I took advantage of her gaze by starting our debate anew, saying that she had me even more worried than before. My job, after all, was to argue strenuously for the status quo.

"Stanley!" Sarah cried. "You really are amazing!"

"Well, let me tell you why I am worried," I began. "Obviously, you did make an independent move, and although it was painful, it was somewhat successful. But I am worried about your mother now, for all the reasons that I have given before. With Sarah successfully making such independent moves, I fear that Miriam will be in jeopardy. I therefore want to make a recommendation to Karl. I think, Karl, that you should follow the tradition of men in this family, of protecting the important ties that their wives have to their children. Therefore, I think you should make every effort to stop Sarah from making any more independent moves." Sarah wailed in disbelief.

"I don't think I can oblige you," Karl said as Sarah shook her head, as if to shake my obvious insanity out of her ears.

Alice declared my recommendation unjustified, as was her prepared position, because she felt my fears were not legitimate. Ruth said that when Sarah made up her mind to be independent, nobody would be able to stop her. I pressed the debate further. "I know that we have disagreed all along," I said to Alice, "but I feel that as the most cautious one among us, I have a responsibility to make this recommendation. I feel strongly about it. I think, Karl, that you really must protect the tie between Miriam and Sarah the way your dad protected the ties in his family. And if you need help in that, you may try consulting your father on it."

Poppa, who was present for this session, quipped, "That's the nicest joke I have heard in two years."

The next session began with Sarah announcing that ". . . immediately after therapy today, I am leaving for Israel." Smiling widely, she looked directly at me for a reaction. Miriam laughed, saying, "She didn't want to call and tell you because she wanted to see your reaction!"

Our expressions must have asked the question "How did this happen?" because Sarah animatedly jumped to answer it.

"Oh, I know what happened!" she yelled. "I know what

happened. Oh, please, Stanley! My mother said, 'This is it! Stanley was right! Stanley is absolutely right!' And she starts crying, and I'm like 'Ma!' And she says, 'I can't talk to your father, and I can't talk to your brother! I'm not allowed to call your sister. You're the only one I can talk to, and I'm going to keep holding on,' and 'How can I do this to you? I am going to destroy both our lives!' and 'Stanley is right!' and 'What are we going to do?' and 'Oh, my God!' ''

When Sarah became calm, Ruth asked her what she planned to do in Israel, but before she could answer, Ruth moved right to the question ''Are you going to visit your mother's family?''

''Oh, my mother already has instructed me firmly on that . . .'' Sarah said.

I shook my head, as if on the verge of commenting sadly.

''. . . that I have to do this also for her,'' Sarah continued, glancing furtively at me.

Miriam interrupted: ''Yes. I told her to be with them, because they need her. Two weeks ago, I called and told them, 'I have a surprise for you. I am sending you my daughter.' My mother said, 'I don't believe it!' She's been very depressed, my mother. Losing a lot of weight. I told her, 'Sarah is coming, so you'll get well.' ''

I shook my head again. Sarah looked at me as if to invite my judgment. I took the cue, saying, ''Sarah, I was very shocked by your telling us that you were going to Israel, because initially I thought it was an independent move. Now, as we talked about it more, I am more reassured—''

''It's dependent,'' she said with fatigue.

''Yes, exactly. I realize now that you are making this trip for your mother, because she needs you to. For some reason, at this moment your mother needs to be reunited with her family, and you are her emissary.''

''Karl,'' Alice said, moving in with another pre-planned suggestion aimed at nurturing the marriage, ''I think *you* are the only one who can bring Miriam together with her parents. I don't think Sarah can do that. That is not going to even the score between you and Miriam, and you know we have a score to even here. You had your parents all these years, and she left hers behind."

We previously had determined this to be a long-standing issue that had helped keep Miriam and Karl apart. After all, it was for Karl's safety that Miriam emigrated and left her family behind. He owed her a reunion, though every time the subject had come up, he had protested the prohibitive cost and said he worried about how he would get along without her while she was gone.

"Never mind," Ruth said, picking up her part as the champion of change. "I think the trip is just fine. I think it is an independent move, whether Stanley thinks so or not. I think it's a great opportunity for you, Sarah, to make whatever decision you have to make, when you are there, to make the trip work for you. It's a great opportunity, though I am aware that it presents a great dilemma, too. If you really were to work on your own behalf and use this opportunity to gain some independence and have a good time, you might decide to stay in Israel a little longer, and there's probably some danger, at least in your head, that if you were to do something like that, you would be putting yourself in the same position in your family that your mother is in hers: going abroad and leaving your family behind."

"We thought of that," Sarah said. "I talked to my mother all night about that. But this is the most independent thing I've ever done in my whole life! C'mon, Stanley, give me credit!"

"I'm afraid I can't."

"Stanley, you're such a damned pessimist!"

"As a matter of fact, Sarah," I said, "I think that your mother needs you very much right now, and I think that if you have to go to extremes to reunite your mother with her family, you should do just that—"

"But what about me? Maybe this is for me!"

"... And if you have to get sick, for example, to the point where your grandparents will have to bring you home, or your mother will have to come and rescue you, then I think you should do it, because your mother needs this reunion."

In order to prove me wrong this time, as she so persistently had in my previous declarations, Sarah would have to succeed on the trip.

And she succeeded, though in a fashion that fell somewhere between a Shakespearean comedy and a grand Italian opera. Sarah of course did get sick at her grandmother's house, groping and writhing and suffering tremendous abdominal pains. After a series of frantic all-night transatlantic telephone marathons and panicky trips to Stamford, Connecticut, for quick passport renewals so that Miriam and Karl could rescue Sarah in Israel, Ari and Ira put pressure on their parents to resist Sarah's lure.

A surprise turning point pivoted on Miriam's mother. She reassured Miriam that Sarah would be all right in her care. "Don't come, at least not now," Miriam's mother told her. "I'll deal with Sarah. I can handle her."

Sarah eventually settled down and enjoyed the trip. Ira remained close to home. Sarah returned from Israel on schedule, and we held a ninth session.

The family arrived looking terribly distressed. Sarah barely could sit through the hour, though we learned that she had returned home on time and full of enthusiasm, talking incessantly of making a permanent move to Israel. Miriam and Karl, meanwhile, had begun to fight about old issues; he was not as kind and as lovable as she would like. She was more critical than he would like. Sarah had become sick again during these marital battles, focusing her parents' attention on her and temporarily putting to rest Miriam and Karl's disagreements.

The most obvious potential consequences of change had risen up and introduced themselves to the family. With Sarah either gone or talking about being gone, Karl and

Miriam had to face each other and their marriage. When Sarah saw how difficult that was, she became ill and dependent again, and thus allowed everyone to evade or postpone a confrontation.

Once again, children failing to keep their parents good parents.

We conducted several separate interviews, though everyone watched. Alice first interviewed Sarah and Ira, exploring the various ways in which Karl helped perpetuate the status quo, letting them know that they were needed at home. Alice then interviewed Karl on the same subject. He denied all of what the children had said about him. He insisted that he wanted finally to be alone with Miriam for their long-deferred honeymoon.

Next, Alice interviewed Miriam, who began by denouncing Karl for not being around when she needed him. "So," she said, "I turn to my children. I go to my kids. What I don't get from him, I get from my kids, even if it's only that they need me. But I can give them what I have to give. With him, I will have anger."

"What do you think he would be afraid of if the children were to leave?" Alice asked.

"I don't know. Maybe he would be depressed. But I was very depressed, and I think it had a lot to do with my parents. I know that my mother has lived her life in depression because she didn't have her children, or she didn't have me, and her life has not been a good life."

"Even when you came to this country?"

"And she never had a great relationship with my father."

"So, the whole time you have been in this country, you have felt responsible for your mother's depression?"

"Right," Miriam answered, wiping an eye.

"And you feel that your father was never able to make that up to her?"

"The whole thing with me is that I left my parents. I took

everything away from them. That's the whole thing. And that comes out all the time for me.''

In this family, we concluded during a short break, another message was that children who leave their parents are responsible for their parents' unhappiness, which made for a double-edged sword of responsibility and failure. You must stay dependent to make your parents good parents, and if ever you leave, you are to blame for their consequent misery.

We decided to have Alice tell Karl that he held the key to unlocking his family's dilemma.

''You have said,'' she began, ''that you want a happy life with Miriam, the two of you alone together. Over all these years, you have given Miriam the children as a consolation prize for having left her family in Israel. She left her family to follow you to this country, and she has been grieving for them ever since. Now, what I'm going to ask you to do is going to be extremely difficult for you. I'm going to ask you to encourage Miriam to return to Israel alone to see her family and settle all the issues that have never been settled.''

Anticipating her father's position, Sarah broke in: ''I have to say I'm going to go on my father's side in this,'' she said, ''because I won't let my mother go to Israel. I'll let her go if I know my grandparents are coming back with her, but if that's not it, I won't let my mother go, and I'll make it very difficult for her to leave.''

Suddenly Sarah was *taking control* of her symptoms, and then threatening to employ them.

I, playing the conservative, said to Karl, ''I think you do hold the key in making the difference in this situation, but I think it's going to be very difficult for you to encourage Miriam to make this very important journey, because to do that would be unfaithful to your own father, who has clearly given you the message that you must help your wife to make the children most important. So to encourage her and to attempt even to find happiness between the two of you is a big risk to you in terms of your own father. I also think you will deeply miss Miriam. That's another reason it will be difficult.''

"Oh, yes," Karl said, "it will be difficult. But I will let her go.''

I turned to Sarah. "But I think, Sarah, you choose to be on your father's side in this, despite the very strong bond you have developed with your mother, because you will do what you have always done, which is to go to whatever extreme necessary—by, say, having these problems—because they will for certain keep your mother from making the trip, and your dad will therefore not have to face the difficult issues in their marriage.''

Alice moved in to disagree with my position, arguing again in favor of the marriage: "Karl, it's up to you to see that Miriam does something for herself and to encourage her to do that. It's really in your best interest." Karl nodded.

In the final session, Miriam declared her independence and said she was preparing to leave for Israel alone. The family reported that Poppa, Karl's father, was angered about the latest developments. "He comes out with little nothings," said Karl, "but they mean a lot. He said, 'What does *she* have to go for?' And 'What are you spending all your money for, anyway? When are you going to stop spending your money?' ''

Alice repeated her encouragement to Karl, saying that when Miriam gets her problems with her parents straightened out, there was a chance she would return to him without the resentment and anger and perhaps rewrite their relationship in much better form. I countered, saying I still did not believe that Karl could disobey his father's wishes by letting Miriam go. Alice said she thought he could. I said Karl had always placed his father first. Alice said she did not think he would do so any longer. "I think he can be a good son *and* a good husband," Alice argued.

Finally, Karl said he was aware of both sides, but he had decided to let Miriam go, and that was that.

Sarah and Ira had transferred much of their concern to their father, and what he would be like if Miriam were away in Israel, but since articulating this concern seemed more directed at making Miriam hesitate about leaving than for any other reason, we separated the two children, and Ruth asked them about it. They were frank about their power now, very cognizant of it. They even toyed with it, knowing that Karl and Miriam were watching through the glass.

"I know this sounds like a way to keep my mother home," Sarah began, "but it really feels like my mother could straighten out a lot of her shit with her parents right here. The other way, with her going, my father is just going to get worse. I know he's going to get worse. There's no doubt in my mind."

"In other words," Ira said with a tone of recently acquired wisdom, "It would be real easy for us to keep her home."

"You two could start openly worrying about your father, for instance," Ruth said.

"All she has to do is sit back there and listen," Sarah said.

"You're doing your number right now, aren't you?" Ruth said.

"Right. Right," Sarah answered. "This is taking care of it. This could do it."

"But now, of course, you understand what a high price your parents have paid for not feeling like good children, particularly your mother. She has suffered tremendously for feeling that she was not a good daughter. And that's been the sorrow of her life. Your father has struggled with it in his way, too. But the two of you have no debts. They had tremendous debts. You don't have any. You're trying to pay debts that you don't have." Ruth looked directly at Ira and asked, "Can you be a spectator in your parents' life for a little while?"

"Sure," Ira said. "Sure. I really have been a good kid."

"That's true," said Ruth. "That's absolutely true. Both of

you have. Sarah, actually, if you want to put it on a scale, has been super. You have been a terrifically good kid, and she's been a super terrific kid.''

Sarah smiled, embarrassed. They had accepted the view. They could free themselves from having to fail to spare their parents misery. They already were good kids and had proved it again and again. They could leave now and live.

Miriam returned to the room, sat down, and bowed her head. ''I can't believe seven years of illness suddenly coming to an end . . .'' she whimpered.

''Well, you watch,'' said Ruth, ''how quickly Sarah is going to get well.''

''I told my mother this morning that I'm going to apply to NYU,'' Sarah said.

We told the Steinmetzes that their therapy was completed.

Both Karl and Miriam had come to therapy with bitter feelings toward their parents for having failed them. They had spent considerable energy over the years trying to show their parents how to be successful parents, mainly by dedicating themselves to their children. Their definition of the system—that good parents solve their children's problems—required a constant escalation of reciprocity. In order to be better parents, they needed increasingly troubled children. The more severe were the children's failures, the more successful the parents could become. Conversely, in order to protect one's parents in this system, a dutiful child would have to fail. With the intensity of this background, it would have to be a dramatic failure, and agoraphobia certainly would be an appropriate choice, given the history. It would also be inevitable for Ira that in finding himself he would find himself back in his family's embrace.

We had turned that system around and placed the emphasis on how high a price Miriam and Karl had paid for not feeling like good children. Miriam shifted her view of herself from the good mother to the bad daughter. But there was hope in that; she could go to Israel and reconcile her role as daughter. In order to stay a good mother, in her system, she would continue to require Sarah, at least, to fail at life. And there wasn't much hope in that.

They returned a year later with a sick and stricken Sarah, suffering this time from severe insomnia. The insomnia had overcome every known chemical combatant prescribed for it. The family had changed dramatically. Ira had left for California, where he had entered in and completed a triathlon. He had found a marginal job that he did not particularly like, but had also decided to stay in California and live there. Sarah had completed a year in NYU and was working full-time in a bookstore. Ari and Marvin had a new baby, further separating them as an independent family unit. Miriam's parents had returned with her from Israel for a prolonged stay, during which they continued the dialogue about their relationship. Miriam also had been diagnosed with a malignant tumor and Karl was showing signs of emotional problems. Again, we were not terribly surprised at that; we actually had predicted Karl's struggle, given the new structure in the family.

Still, they had returned to us because they wanted help for Sarah. It took only minutes with Ruth for Sarah to concede, with an engaging smile of both discovery and relief, that by contracting severe insomnia, by getting so sick again, that her parents had to bring her back to therapy, *she* had in fact brought her *parents* to therapy. Karl still struggled with breaking from his father. He and Miriam now had a family with comparatively successful children. Their needs had changed. But still, here was Sarah, back again, being the super-good kid. Ruth asked her, ''Can you turn your parents over to us now, for therapy, and go on with your own life?''

She said she could. At least this time, she hadn't suffered for seven years to help her parents; she'd brought them for help.

As far as we know, she slept that night.

POSTSCRIPT

Over years of treating families of Holocaust survivors, I have discovered—and the experiences of other professionals repeatedly has affirmed for me—that the families seem to reorganize in two distinct ways as a result of this trauma: either they refuse to talk about it, or they talk about it incessantly. There are consequences that are traceable to each.

In some families, the experience, with its grief and pain, is veiled in silence and remains a great mystery to the children of the first generation, who realize early in their lives that all members of the family have tacitly agreed that any attempt to define the past is dangerous and must be avoided. Consciously or subconsciously they are warned to avoid it—which, of course, makes it an ever-present gap, a looming and crucially important nonentity.

In these families, when the second and third generation members develop symptoms, the symptoms tend to relate to the lack of definition of reality. For instance, in one case, a second generation child had developed psychotic-like behavior that became extremely exacerbated whenever the therapeutic team began to probe the family's history. The child's behavior became bizarre at these definable junctures, so we prescribed that she do what she already was doing, but we gave it a structure where none previously had existed. We suggested that the child stay in the other room as the therapy progressed, and we asked her to bang on the observation mirror when she thought the conversation was getting dangerous. Every time the parents started to talk about the past and their guilt, disappointment, shame, and loss, the daughter went wild, banging on the mirror. Eventually, and after many complicated maneuvers, the parents realized what their daughter was doing. They told her that they didn't need her to do it anymore; they would be all right, they would talk about their past. Eventually, the daughter was reassured, and the therapy continued without her interruptions.

In the "Holocaused" case, we had a classic example of a family who refused to let go of the past. Holding on to the past becomes a central, organizing fact in such families—they think about the losses, abandonments, betrayals, separations, and mysteries, talk about them constantly, either directly or metaphorically, practically live and breathe them. In these families, we frequently see members of the older generations holding on to younger members tenaciously, refusing to let them go. The children and grandchildren develop symptoms, tending to reflect this dynamic by way of separation anxiety, agoraphobia and the sorts of psychosomatic illness that would keep a child at home.

The Steinmetz case obviously was typical of this category. Because of the extreme nature of Sarah's psychosomatic illness and her agoraphobia, and because of the history of failure in prior therapy, we felt from the beginning that a radical approach was necessary. We three therapists reconstructed ourselves as a family, echoing the different voices in the Steinmetz family. Also, we mirrored the close involvement among family members by similarly becoming intensely involved in our own debate, allowing conflict among ourselves and showing the Steinmetzes that we could differ and still function as a family. Thus, we used their own hidden messages to show what they were doing but had been unable to recognize.

I frankly delighted in my role in the therapeutic approach. As the only male member of the therapy team, I was to adopt the position of a family member opposed to change, a posture that would not normally be mine. Yet, we agreed that I would present that opinion and argue for it as convincingly as if it were my own, while my colleagues provided counterpoints, arguing the other facets of the dilemma. "Keep your symptoms, Sarah," I would argue. "It's too dangerous for you to be well. You're actually fairly

safe if everything stays this way, and so is everyone else.''
So, for me, the tension and anxiety generated by the real
drama of serious therapy was secretly ameliorated by an
exhilarating challenge that floated somewhere between
scripted stage-acting and debate-team improvisation. In
overlapping ironies, I was performing as an actor in a real-
life drama.

I got the clear and endearing impression—reinforced over
and over again whenever I view the videotapes—that Sarah,
of all people, was seeing through the tactic while simultaneously allowing it to work by suspending her disbelief just
as she might in the theater. She somehow knew that I was
being different from who I am; yet she went along with it.
I sensed, too, that my ''bad boy'' routine had a seductive
effect on her. She kidded about my intransigence, smiling
now and then, as if she knew and appreciated that it was
all part of an act of counterbalance. She seemed charmed
by the knowledge that we knew that she was in control,
protecting her family by staying symptomatic. She seemed
proudly amused by the notion that she could prove me (or
my therapeutic persona) wrong by changing and equally
amused by the knowledge that my real persona favored and
applauded each of her strides.

It was a very rewarding case, and I often think about that
family, because while our therapy relieved much of Sarah's
terrible suffering, the pain did not disappear; it redistrib-
uted itself. Sarah had unconsciously volunteered self-
sacrificially to suffer the bulk of her family's residual burden
of history. When she finally abdicated her disproportionate
share of the responsibility, her parents and siblings had to
pick up theirs. We ended the therapy when we were confident that Sarah was on her way to self-liberation, freed of
the need to be so painfully symptomatic—though she remained available to the family, symptoms and all, for such
times of crisis as they encountered a year later. When Miriam's cancer revealed itself, for instance, Sarah stood by to

absorb the family's anxiety by returning to her symptoms, this time, consciously enough to steer them to therapy.

Once again, though, we were left with numbing realization that the waste from history's atrocities lingers for generations.

GETTING CRAZY

Buffalo, New York, Winter 1986

MYRNA NOVIK WAS DESCRIBED TO ME AS AN OVERWEIGHT, quite crazy thirty-four-year-old woman who had been under regular treatment for more than half her life. At a combination seminar and consultation in her native Buffalo, where I was lecturing and consulting once a month at a church-affiliated counseling center, a participating psychologist told me: "She's the senior member here. She has more seniority than the staff. They come and go; she remains."

I asked for a brief outline of her background and got a litany of bleak facts in return. The daughter of a man who had spent vast portions of his life in psychiatric institutions, and who in fact was in one at that very moment, Myrna had been molested by an uncle when she was barely pubescent and raped again by a stranger when she was fifteen years old.

The second rape produced her first child, who had Down's syndrome. Doctors and county officials advised that she institutionalize the baby, and Myrna declined. They insisted; she refused. In the ensuing years, Myrna had married three times, her selections crossing racial lines for her second and third husbands. Her third husband, with whom she lived when I met her, was unemployed and collecting a small monthly disability allowance from Social Security Supplemental Security Income. All three children were of mixed racial ancestry, inasmuch as the assailant who had sired her first child was of African descent also.

The psychologists at the center considered Myrna ''impossibly irresponsible,'' partly for insisting from the outset that she maintain custody of the Down's syndrome child, partly because she had an apparently uncontrollable penchant for shoplifting, and probably also because she had twice broken unspoken taboos against miscegenation.

Her shoplifting was the most often stated reason, though. She had been caught at it numerous times and once had even gotten herself sentenced to weekends in the city jail. Therapists complained year after year that they could not seem to make her understand that her risking further incarceration by continuing to indulge in compulsive thievery was effectively equivalent to abandoning her children. She was therefore openly abdicating her responsibility as a mother. ''Irresponsible and crazy,'' they called her.

Accidentally, I caught sight of Myrna before our formal introduction, while another staff member was tactfully advising her of my arrival and my intended advisory role in her therapy. I was quite surprised at Myrna's demeanor, particularly her woefully drawn facial expression. I had half expected to see someone flighty and frivolous, perhaps overly adorned in fake jewelry and excessive makeup, or someone disheveled and reeking of self-neglect.

Myrna's round face was framed in long straight brown hair, not unkempt but not ostensibly attended to. She wore a polyester blue blouse, its shirttail draped outside the waistline of her black slacks. She wore black canvas slip-on sneakers, shoes that were comfortable, functional, inexpensive, and unostentatious—very practical. She was overweight, but in her face was the faint suggestion that she might once have been a beautiful child, if not a beautiful young woman. Her facial muscles seemed taut and strained, as if they were weighted down by a gravitational pull stronger than that affecting most other people. I watched through the one-way glass as she sat in a metal-backed chair and waited for me with her feet crossed and her hands in her lap.

I studied the face.

Myrna's head leaned over to the right in the manner of a dazed prizefighter's. Her ready frown reflected the drawn shape of her cheeks above and her brow above them, forming chevrons of burdened sadness. She did not look crazy and irresponsible. She looked worn, exhausted, and perilously close to defeated.

I introduced myself and said I had heard a lot about her. She snorted, as if to say that whatever I had heard, it probably was all bad. The reaction was like that of a child in the principal's office for the fifteenth time, only this time with a new principal. When I said that I'd heard a lot about her, Myrna "knew" the deck already was stacked against her. I felt instantly that I had taken a step backward.

So, I thought I would surprise her. Instead of asking questions, I began the session by telling her what I knew about her—that she had three children, one of them with Down's syndrome; that she was taking care of her husband and her sick mother as well; and that she had been caring for her mother since she was a teenager. I said I knew that she was not getting any child support from her ex-husbands and had to rely on Social Services and her wits to keep everybody for whom she was responsible clothed, fed, and reasonably well cared for.

She nodded slowly as I spoke. Finally I said, "I don't understand how you manage to do all that. It seems like a great deal of work and responsibility."

An observing therapist later remarked on how I had begun the process of reversing Myrna's self-perception by manipulating the information she had given me. I may have begun this process, but there was no clever, manipulative tactic to my approach. My admiration and sympathy were real.

"It's just real hard," she responded, weakened by the

unexpected understanding. "Life is just real hard. I think I was really . . . I was not prepared for it. I was just not prepared for how hard it was."

I learned later that the experienced observers in the anteroom were surprised at both her statement and the tone of resignation with which she had delivered it. It was as if they were seeing her tired for the first time. When she said life was hard, she closed her eyes with an emphasis laden with difficulty and pain.

"It makes me mad," she said, "because I'm learning that I could have done things differently. But yet, when I think about what I could do, when I think about what I can do now, it just freezes me in place." She clenched her hands together. "So therefore, I'm just content to be in the confines of my home. Like other stuff isn't there." She waved her hands, as if waving other things away.

A smoker in those days, I reached for a cigarette.

"You may be thinking about the wrong things to do," I said. "It sounds like you're trying harder to be more responsible."

I was thinking about the phrase "Irresponsible and crazy," her label, and how supremely responsible she appeared to me, practically from childhood; and then how she seemed never to have had enough time or freedom to relax, or even to go a little crazy.

"So, how would it be if you went crazy?" I asked. "It sounds like great fun to me."

Sadly, turning away to the right, she said, "It does."

The sadness convinced me that I was on the right track. Not only did she need to go crazy, she knew she needed it. Anyone else might have chuckled at such a suggestion, thinking it was a joke, coming from a therapist. For Myrna, "great fun" was no joke. It was the Impossible Dream. She then added, "Well, my sister, underneath me, and a lot of other people, say that it's a cheap way out. It's a coward's way out, and maybe that's what keeps me from not doing it. It was my *father's* way out."

The statement startled me for its perception. Her father was institutionalized. Who would think of institutionalization as a way out of anything? Someone who was stuck with the leftover responsibilities, no doubt.

"How did he do it?" I asked. "What did he pick?"

"He just went berserk on religion," she said. "He just brought religion as the main focus to take care of some guilt that he had as a child. It played into his whole life."

"Was your mother the responsible one?"

"Yeah. Well . . . she was more responsible than my father. She wasn't as responsible as I would have liked."

"But you were more like her than like your father. You were closer to her?" I was challenging the perception that she was following in her father's "crazy" footsteps.

"Well, I was closer because she was the one that was there more of the time. He would have to go to the hospital and stay there a lot of times. And then when he *was* there, he was working."

Thinking of her father's periodic hospitalization, I said, "You mean he was allowed vacation time."

"He allowed himself vacation. That's for sure!" she said.

"He sounds like a wise man," I said, having just figured out exactly what I was going to do and to recommend. "Now, when was the last time *you* had a vacation?" I asked. "The last time you remember letting go?"

"I guess I let myself go when I go and steal," she said. She tilted her head left, toward me, and looked up at me in a shy, childlike manner. "They told you about my stealing?" she asked with lips pursed like Shirley Temple.

"Yes."

"Yeah," she said, returning to her sadness. "That . . . to me that's a kick. To me that makes me feel good, something that I feel I do for myself, but . . . I guess what I have to learn is how to channel doing things for myself in a better way, so that it doesn't end up making me feel worse or something." She looked up at me for approval. She had put no feeling into the last statement; it just sounded like a statement a therapist would want to hear. She knew a lot about therapists.

"Are you good at it? Stealing?"

"Real good!" she said with a slight laugh. "Too good."

"Tell me how do you do it. Maybe I could learn a lesson or two."

"You could. I wish . . . I have a sister trying to tell me I should turn it around and use it to make money by trying to teach stores how to make their security better. It sounded good at the time. It sounded like something that someday could probably be really real. But I've never—I've never acted on it."

"But you're an expert."

"I'm not an expert, but I'm among the best. I'm *not* an expert, and I have been caught, many times."

"Have you been to jail? Have you managed to stay out of jail?"

"I had to do a month of weekends one time. That was the only incarceration I had, other than just being there until you get to court."

"Well, that's one way of taking a vacation, isn't it? On the other hand, you're such an extremely responsible person! How does someone who is so responsible, and so concerned about her children, her mother, her husband, how do you ever get the opportunity to let go unless you find someone to help you achieve that?"

I excused myself, saying I wanted to talk with my colleagues. In the room, I told them how diametrically opposite she looked to me from what I had heard about her. I also suggested, carefully, that I had a different view of Myrna's refusing to institutionalize her Down's syndrome baby. Their contention was that institutionalization would have been a more responsible act. "Just from the way she looks and the amount of work she has to do," I said, "I think Myrna saw abandoning the baby as an escape from responsibility. Where did we get the idea that this woman was irresponsible?"

"What about the shoplifting?" an observer asked. "I mean, she doesn't just steal things; she steals according to a list."

"What do you mean, a list?" I asked.

"She goes shoplifting with a list of items to steal. She doesn't just pick a necklace here and a gold watch there. She's not merely out of control for a moment or for ten minutes; she goes in specifically to steal specific things, things other people have ordered."

"And she gives the things to these people?" I asked.

"Worse. They pay her for them."

"And what does she do with the money?"

"What difference does it make what she does with the money?"

"Do you know what she does with it?"

"Well, she doesn't go to Las Vegas with it, if that's what you're suggesting."

"I'm sorry. I didn't mean to suggest anything. My feeling is that her stealing in this fashion might be consistent with her responsible behavior."

"Stealing as responsible behavior?"

"The way you describe it," I said, "she does it as a business. How irresponsible was Dickens's Fagin? His boys went to work every day picking pockets. It was a skill, and in an economy where they had no other work. They rehearsed their moves, went through mock drills. For that, they all got fed and housed, and they survived. Unless there's some evidence to the contrary, I suspect that the proceeds of Myrna's excursions go to augment the cost of supporting her mother and her family. That's pretty responsible behavior, it seems to me. It's risky, certainly, because it's against the law. She's risking jail. We're learning a lot here. Myrna is no classic kleptomaniac. She evidently isn't impulsive; she's purposeful. She doesn't need to be more responsible. If anything, she needs a break. Maybe that's it. Maybe what she needs is a day off. Time when she is not responsible for all these people. So far, weekends in jail are the only vacation she's had."

I returned to the room.

"Have a fantasy," I said, "about what you would do if you were to go crazy with me today. What would you do if we were to make this our vacation, free from all responsibilities?"

"Talking," she said quietly. "Maybe going somewhere. Sightseeing in the city or something, some points of interest. And still have communication going. I think that's a way of—"

"That's so responsible! You're going to show me Buffalo?"

She thought about it for two seconds and seemed to determine that sightseeing in Buffalo was not that crazy after all. She would have to come up with something really wild. "I'd probably end up going all the way," she said, employing a phrase from another era. To make herself clear, she added, and this time very demurely, "I'd probably . . . we'd end up sexually involved."

Of course, I thought. *Still responsible. The perfect tour guide. If you were to go absolutely crazy and be totally irresponsible; if you were to let go completely and have the wildest time of your life, you might do it by showing a man around Buffalo and then making love to him.*

I excused myself again.

"I don't know if you noticed," I told those watching, "but earlier in our session, Myrna gave me the tool that I was looking for to use as my intervention in this case, as my way of moving her to look at herself in a different way, to look at her life in a different way and maybe handle it differently as a result. She told it to me almost as if she knew it all along. And in a profound way I believe that she did know it all along, but needed someone to encourage her. I find that frequently. The patient knows better than anybody what he needs to do for himself and is merely searching for someone to encourage him to do it. I plan to do that in the next few moments. I'm going to give Myrna Novik an assignment, and when I do, for those of you who haven't already figured out what my plan is, I want you to think about the degree of honor and respect that inspires it, because honor and respect are fundamental to what we are trying to do."

I returned to the conference room with Myrna.

"It is rare," I said, "that I meet somebody as responsible as you are, somebody who tries so hard to keep things in order. If you continue to steal, although you're an expert at it—"

"Not an expert," she interrupted humbly.

"Well, good at it, a good one. But now that you mention it, if your unconscious longing is to let go, you will never become an expert, and you will get caught. If you have an unconscious longing, as I'm sure you do . . ."

"To take a holiday?" she guessed correctly.

". . . to take a holiday," I agreed, "you *will* get caught and be forced to take a holiday. So, I think you need lessons in how to let go. And I think there is only one teacher in the world for you . . ."

I paused.

". . . and that is your father," I said. "He seems to be a master at it."

Myrna closed her eyes. The corners of her mouth rose slightly, forming a resigned, relaxed grin, as if she not only agreed but was genuinely relieved and gladdened to hear the suggestion.

"So my advice to you is to make a visit to your father and to ask him to teach you how to let go. 'Dad, you have something that I have not allowed myself to have, and something that maybe I haven't appreciated about you. You have a gift for taking holidays. You have an ability to let go, to unburden yourself.' "

"He does," she said.

" 'And I want you to teach me this,' " I continued, pausing again.

Her eyes moistened. I thought that she might have been moved by the mere possibility of momentary relief—from the burdens of her daily life, from whatever burden she felt about her relationship with her father, from the burden of clinic staff members telling her over and over that she was irresponsible when she knew she was the opposite.

I waited a moment.

"So, Myrna, could I trust that you will visit him and take from his wisdom those lessons, and use them in a way that would give you the opportunity to unburden yourself just a bit? Can you do that?"

"Yes," she said. "I can do that."

"I think your father might be honored."

"That I would ask him? He probably would be."

"And you might even feel less guilty about having been so oppositional with him, so rebellious."

She nodded, unable to speak.

Later, I discussed Myrna Novik's case in a seminar. My recognition of and respect for her sense of responsibility— in the face of years of accusations of irresponsibility—had rattled certain of the observers' prejudices. Some no doubt would cling to their former notions (responsible shoplifting, indeed!). I wouldn't say that the concept overwhelmed them, but it turned their dial to a different channel for a while. I had the sense, though, that whereas they had seemed competitively threatened by my approach, they now were more intellectually curious. Some even seemed emotionally excited by what had been accomplished and, moreover, by their participation in it.

Described as a failure, as her father was similarly described, Myrna had viewed herself as a failure and her family as a family of failures. Our encounter structured a different view, that of a woman who was successful at assuming and meeting responsibilities. Moreover, Myrna had rejected her father for what she viewed as his failures, but the intervention placed him in a position of success, too— as an expert at letting go, as someone quite in charge of his so-called irresponsibility, even to the point of getting himself incarcerated when he felt the world was too much for him. In a way, he had the better idea for letting go, because he was in control of his incarcerations. She was risking a forced rest that might come at an inconvenient time. At any rate, the intervention was intended to repair Myrna's view of herself, and it repaired her view of her father as well. A bonus, in my book.

One observing therapist wondered aloud what would happen next. The answer was anyone's guess, but I presented this possible scenario: if Myrna consulted her father as prescribed, there existed a chance that she could repair her relationship with him. First, she would be honoring him, thus changing the past and providing a different foundation for a different future. Then? Perhaps he might offer her an alternative to the idea of incarceration. He might have good advice for her. He might feel freed to offer her help. I couldn't know that. I knew only that she had left the premises with a different view of herself and of him, and therefore with new options and new hope.

POSTSCRIPT

Surprise creates a momentary rupture in the thought process. The mind, momentarily confused, is thrown off balance, and in that rare moment, the opportunity arises to introduce a new thought. As a therapist, I use surprise as a technique, a means of disrupting a pattern of thinking and creating a moment of attention in which I can introduce a new idea. In the case of Myrna Novik, not only did I use it with the patient but with an entire agency which was watching me, confident in the ascription of hopelessness they had made.

As luck would have it, well-meaning guardians of tradition had so completely misunderstood Myrna Novik that the entire clinical audience got to witness a total reversal of therapeutic direction—and in a single surprising session. Even the most skeptical observers were buzzing about the case at the end of the day, and everyone confessed to having gained a new perspective on their old standby—their ever-present, "crazy," and "irresponsible" patient, Myrna the shoplifter.

As a therapist, I had the incalculable satisfaction of giving a surprisingly new view and new hope to a deeply conflicted but fundamentally fine person. As a performer, I had the thrill of pleasing all segments of an audience to one degree or another. As a representative of a school of thought that challenged tradition, I won some converts. As a teacher, I had offered a perspective on behavior opposite from tradition, in tandem with presenting the possibility that a patient might not have a problem at all but a solution to a problem.

Myrna's case provided me with a living, breathing illustration of my point, and then some. Her demeanor told me she was burdened by some responsibility long before her words did. And wasn't it enough that she had suffered abuse, abandonment, and emotional and economic poverty—did she also merit society's condemnation for its own betrayal of her? How criminal of us to call irresponsible someone who in a very calculated way systematically accepted daily responsibility for all the people around her.

Because Myrna's calculated way of coping was criminal, though, I was walking on eggs, so to speak, when I suggested its value to her. I had to be ever careful to convey respect for her responsible motivations for her activity but not for the activity itself. I never suggested that she engage in it, though I tried to bring it under her control. And, in offering as a possible explanation for her taking such chances that she was always risking a forced vacation from responsibility, I posed the notion of taking a rest from responsibility without the risk of incarceration.

I don't know that this would have been a one-shot intervention had I not been a visiting teacher-therapist on a show-and-tell mission to a distant city. I might have wanted at least another session with Myrna, if only to support her altered perspective and her I hope changed relationship with her father, whose tradition she genuinely followed—though ironically with less control than he.

Assuming I would not see Myrna again, I took comfort in the wider impact that the session had on the agency, wherein everyone's definition of a problem got turned inside out. Everyone, including Myrna, was forced to rethink moral issues and psychological issues and to reexamine their own patterns of thought regarding problems and solutions. Myrna had bought the family's definition of her father as crazy just as the agency had bought society's definition of Myrna as crazy. The intervention offered the agency a different way of thinking about her; it offered Myrna a different way of thinking about herself and her father, a way that permitted her to short-circuit her rebellion from him and lessen her overidentification with her mother. Moreover, the case raised the question of craziness in general, and irresponsibility. Who was crazy, after all? The father? Myrna? The agency? Her last three therapists?

Me?

THE PATIENT
WHO CURED
HIS THERAPIST

STARTING WITH THE PREMISE THAT FAILURES OFTEN ARE QUITE functional, we can see that an apparent impasse in any kind of relationship often can be found to be accomplishing some yet undefined, undetermined purpose. When called upon by a colleague therapist, for instance, to help with a therapeutic relationship that she considered a failure, I was inclined to try to discover what such a failure could be accomplishing. As always, the discovery wrought surprises.

Buffalo, New York, Winter 1986

Judy Reed had been seeing Tom Martin on and off for two or three years. She told me that she had been stymied by what she saw as his steadfast refusal to reveal himself to her, to trust her, to open up and communicate with her. She had tried everything, she said, and she predicted that within minutes I would see what she meant. I would be confronted with an obviously intelligent, articulate, and fairly well-educated man who would converse in monotonic monosyllables, and at a pace that would have me squirming. Dark-eyed and slender, Judy was intense, articulate, and eager. Initially I was excited by her enthusiasm for the work. She did not appear to be offering me her most frustrating case to test me; she seemed truly desperate to help her client. "He is simply the most withdrawn person I have ever encountered," she said. "No man is an island? This man is an island!"

Because she was so graphically convincing in her description, I had to step away for a few moments before the session began. I felt I had to erase some of the strength of her impressions from my mind. Later, I attempted to explain that seemingly odd, meditative departure to some assembled student therapists, wondering all the while if they considered me crazy.

I told them that once, while I was seated in the living room of an apartment, waiting for a friend to shower and dress, I had amused myself by staring at a crimson Christmas stocking hanging from his mantel. Emblazoned in neat script at the top of the stocking was his son's first name, Paul, written in sprinkles of silvery confetti. I noticed that I could not look at the script without my mind forming the imaginary "sound" of the word *Paul*. I tried to force myself to see the symbols otherwise. What would "Paul" look like to me if I had just landed from another planet with another kind of written language, and I had never seen such symbols before?

The first symbol was like a tree leaning to the right, its boughs and branches growing only on its right side. The tree's root proceeded in that direction, too, from ground level and then upward to the top of an adjacent short, round bush. It also leaned to the right, as did every symbol following. Connected from the second symbol's bottom were two similarly short, vertical symbols of growth, as I tried to view them. They were connected from their bases to each other, and finally to another right-leaning tree that bore no branches or boughs.

The exercise was nearly impossible, because my knowledge and memory of the word *Paul* kept getting in my way. I knew that the symbols existed apart from my knowledge and assumptions, but it seemed that I could not make myself see them without associating them with the sound Paul. Eventually I did it, but only for a fraction of a second. I saw "Paul" as an interesting scribble, unhampered by prior knowledge or prior impressions. I saw the symmetry of the symbols, their directional preference, their liquidity, their individuality, and their interdependence. They seemed like a scouting party of hieroglyphics, headed eastward under the leadership of their stoutest member. Then *Paul* jumped back into my head, and it was over. I could not retrieve it again.

I said I found it to be an exciting exercise and recommended that they try it some time, with numbers, with symbols, with people. An exercise in erasing crippling assumptions, it would both force and allow them to view a problem entirely differently, and I was about to do exactly that.

In preparation for my visit, and as standard protocol for visiting clinical lecturers, Judy Reed had suggested to her patient that their protracted impasse might best be served by a second opinion. She had asked if he would be willing to participate in a consultation with a therapist from New York City who would be visiting as part of a clinical-teaching seminar. After asking for details about what exactly would take place and hearing her explanation that it would be a session observed by her and her colleagues and would possibly be of benefit to him and everyone else, Tom Martin consented.

He entered the room. I sat opposite him, my back to the two-way glass. I told him we would be videotaped if he didn't mind. He nodded his head toward the left very slightly, and raised one eyebrow almost imperceptibly in a gesture that I took to mean a contraction of a shrug, which in turn meant either "No problem" or "If it's my permission you want, you've got it." Dark-eyed, he had a receding hairline that emphasized a pleasant, roundish face, one you might expect to see on a priest or a pharmacist.

He sat down, crossed his legs, placed his hands in his lap, and seemed for all the world to be comfortable. I asked him how he felt. He shrugged and said, "Fine," and then after a pause, added, "Thank you." We laughed together at his belated politeness. I asked how long he had been coming to the center for sessions; he answered, "Several years, on and off. Two years." I asked how he had started, what had prompted his coming in the first place.

"My girlfriend brought me here," he said.

Right away I had a therapist experiencing difficulty communicating with a patient who had not come to her with any problem of his own. The patient's girlfriend had brought him to the center. What was her problem?

"Why? Why do you think she brought you?" I asked.

"She doesn't feel that I communicate well. I guess I don't talk to her enough about how I feel."

So far he was merely telling me what he thought he ought to be telling me. The easy trap would have been for me to then ask how he felt. If he didn't tell me, his girlfriend and his therapist and I would all be in the same predicament. But instead I asked, "What happens when you don't express yourself?"

"She gets angry with me," he said. "She tries harder."

"Well, then what happens? What do you do next?"

He paused for a long time. As it turned out, this was the answer to my question. She tried to get him to express himself, and he paused. She tried harder; he paused longer. That frustrated her, and not only her.

"I don't know what to do," he said finally. "She's angry, and I'm the cause."

"Do you get angry in response?"

"No," he said calmly. "But I feel bad."

"You feel that you're disappointing her," I declared.

He paused again, but contemplatively, not artificially, not frozen with dread or muted by shame or confusion. He was taking his time, thinking about the suggestion. I waited. The silence in the room seemed long but not threatening.

Most patients would have felt obligated to break it. Tom did not. He was content to think, and I was curious enough not to interrupt him. He seemed serene. He *was* serene.

After ten seconds or so, he said, ''Yeah.''

Now *I* let some time pass. I would share in his tempo, his pace. I found it increasingly remarkable that this man felt no uneasiness during any of the vast lulls in our talk. He wasn't trying to impress anyone. He wasn't trying to convince anyone. He seemed to feel no social needs, to harbor no anxieties about what I might have been thinking. It was not as uncomfortable as I might have thought it would be, either, although I am certain that it presented a problem to the observers, especially Judy, Tom's therapist. If his serenity bothered his girlfriend, and possibly Judy, as well, now here, were *two* serene men. One was believed to have a problem that required fixing; the other was the expert called in to fix it.

The therapist who had framed Tom as withdrawn now had a dilemma. In deciding to meet Tom on his own wavelength, I also was deciding—and, in fact, declaring—that it was not bad to be this kind of man. I was conscious of it at the moment I entered his universe. It became very clear to me that I was not going the active route that his therapist had taken; she had focused on qualities she saw as opposite hers. I was finding sameness, respecting Tom's absolute calm. I didn't know what I was going to do yet, but I could see what was going on, and I could actually experience the depth of his serenity. Then, of course, I began wondering why a therapist in the face of such a peaceful man would want him to be otherwise. Maybe *she* had a problem.

Tom's universe, by the way, was much less pressured than ours. I enjoyed my time in it. If he felt no obligation to fill the temporal spaces between questions and answers, there was no need to me to feel any. It became fairly relaxing, in a way, and peaceful.

''Are you disappointing her?'' I asked after some time. Another long pause before he said, ''I don't know.''

"Could it be that she doesn't appreciate you?"

He looked down and to the right, in further contemplation, almost as if he were puzzled by this "new" notion: that his girlfriend's problem with him could be hers and not his, that his therapist's problem could be her own, too. I let another five seconds go by without a response and then said, "You seem quite serene to me."

Long pause. "I do?"

Short pause (I wasn't quite as serene). "You do."

The pace must have been driving the observers nutty.

He paused again, then said, "I've had a lot of practice"—a remark whose significance absolutely slipped by me until much later.

"It's puzzling to me," I said, "because I don't know why you would want to change that. I don't know why anybody would want to be less comfortable or less serene."

Gigantic pause.

"So, how is it that people, or at least women, don't understand what kind of man you are?" I asked. "You're extremely sensitive to what other people think?"

"Quite a bit, yeah."

"Well, that clarifies something for me."

"What does it clarify?" He was suddenly curious.

"Well, my experience with you, which has been brief, is that you are a man endowed with some wonderful qualities. You are content, serene. You are generous, to the degree that you care so much about how your behavior disturbs your girlfriend, you have come to therapy sessions for two years. Yet the woman you live with does not appreciate those things about you. And somehow you have accepted that their view of you is better than your own view of you."

I stopped. He pondered. Another ten or fifteen seconds passed. He rubbed his forefinger under his nose. He stared down and to the right. At length he said:

"Could be."

"What is your view of the therapy that has happened so far?" I asked. "It's been a long time. Two years."

Huge pause. He did not want to say to a therapist that therapy was a waste of time, though I suspect he felt it was.

"Are you addicted to it?" I asked.

"To the weekly counseling sessions? I don't know," he said, lapsing into more deliberation. "It's an interesting question. I never thought of it. I haven't thought of myself as addicted to it. I don't know."

"Is Judy Reed addicted to you? You know, your therapist?"

"I don't know. Maybe she is."

"You have some suspicion to that effect."

"Possibly. Yeah."

"What would make you think that?"

"Maybe because she sought me to participate in this consultation. Maybe she wants . . . maybe she's addicted to her desire to see a change in me."

Another long pause. I knew what I was going to do now. I thought of Judy's description of him, one of frustration, not one of respect. Neither his girlfriend nor his therapist respected or appreciated this man. They had failed him and had then accused him of failing them; and convincingly, too, evidently. The therapist's failure was simple: she merely took over the job of the girlfriend in not respecting Tom Martin and in insisting that he behave differently. In effect, the girlfriend had said, "You need help in being the person I want you to be. I will introduce you to a professional person who agrees with me, and she will help you fix yourself so that you can more closely resemble my idea of you."

A popular psychological myth declares that it is always better to be an expressive person, not to be withdrawn or retiring. In many cases, this is how women want men to be, and how therapists want patients to be. And in many cases, I'm sure it *is* better to be expressive. For Tom Martin, however, that would have been alien. It simply was not him.

"It's sad, isn't it?" I said, referring to Judy's addiction.

"If it were true, it might be. I don't know if it's true."

"Well," I ventured, "how are you going to cure your therapist?" I wanted to tell him that not only was he all right, but in his serene kindness he was serving needs in both his girlfriend and his therapist.

He grinned, but he thought about the question. "Cure her from what?" he asked. "Trying to change me?"

"Precisely."

"I don't know," he said, grinning again.

"Can *you* be *her* therapist?" I asked him.

"I don't think so."

"I think she needs to be cured by you."

"If and when I cure her, then what?"

"Then she won't need you anymore. Then perhaps she'll understand what a lovely man you are."

"How do I cure her?"

"Well, suppose I bring her in, and you give it a try." I waited, and then added, "You're a very competent man. You can rely on your creativity and your competence. I think that you can find ways in which to let those important people in your life know what kind of man you are, what fine qualities you are endowed with."

"What would that do for me?" he asked. "How will that make me feel better?"

"Don't you want to be appreciated?"

He did not answer. I decided it was time to do something, and I rose and announced that I would go outside to the observers' room and invite Judy Reed in. I said that he would be her therapist instead of the other way around. She seemed nervously amused at the idea. In fact, everybody in the observers' room seemed nervous. The tables had turned. It was clear that Tom had become a stand-in for a character in his therapist's life.

We watched as Judy sat in my chair and waited for Tom to speak.

"I'm supposed to cure you," he said, eliciting a burst of laughter from two people in the room with me. Tom laughed, too. "How long have you been having these problems?" he joked, to more laughter.

"Mr. Siegel says that you have an addiction to me, that you don't appreciate me. You don't appreciate my fine qualities: I'm serene and I'm comfortable, and you must not appreciate that, because you're trying to change that, to change me. And there is another person who tried, who also does not appreciate me: my girlfriend."

Tom put his hands together, fingertips to fingertips, as if in prayer.

His analysis was perfect, as far as I was concerned: the perfect dilemma presented by the idea of change. He was content with himself; they were not. If he were to make them happy, he would have to change. If he changed, he might not be content anymore.

"So, I'm going to cure you," he continued. "I don't know how. You know, a lot of people would love to be as comfortable as I am, or at least as comfortable as I sometimes appear to be—"

She nodded in agreement. "I think I'm becoming aware of that," she said, "aware that you're a lot more comfortable. I think that I probably misjudged you, or didn't see it."

Long pause. Tom was openly communicating with one of the women who had been trying unsuccessfully to get him to do just that. Paradoxically, in explaining the potential perils of change, he was changing.

"You don't appreciate me," he said.

"Why not?" she asked, trying to regain her former role.

"Why do you not appreciate me?" he said, suggesting by his tone that only she could answer the question. I thought, "Nice move, Tom." In the room where I sat, there were many stunned faces. Not only was Tom expressing himself, he was openly challenging his therapist's persistent negative view of him.

"I guess because I thought you should be different," she said. "Maybe in some ways, not be so serene."

"The whole Alcoholics Anonymous prayer is based on serenity," he said, startling me.

"Alcoholics Anonymous!" I said, out of earshot. I turned to one of the observers familiar with the case history, Linda Duly, a colleague in Judy's study group.

"Tom Martin is in AA?" I asked.

"Yes, for some years," she said. "This is pretty remarkable what's happening here. You probably also ought to know, given the circumstances, that Judy's husband doesn't talk to her very much and that it troubles her deeply. In fact, her marriage is pretty tense right now. In fact—God, it's all shaping up—according to Judy, her father is as withdrawn and distant as Tom Martin appears to be. That distance always has been a problem in Judy's family. In our study group—where we examine each other's family dynamics—Judy revealed that at an early age she became her mother's ally in trying to get the father more involved with the family. What's becoming clear to me is that Judy appears to have recreated the same relationship with her husband as her mother had with her father, and then recreated it again here with this patient. It's really amazing."

"She's very consistent, isn't she?" I said.

Linda looked at me quizzically but fondly as well. "Your cup is always half full, isn't it?" she said.

I said I viewed Judy as someone who was constantly trying to repair a ruptured relationship from her past, someone who was therefore always hopeful, always patient, because she was still trying to repair an old relationship. "If she's still trying," I said, "then somehow she must still believe that it can be repaired and that it is worth the effort. I'm not reading that positiveness into the situation, either. I'm quite convinced that it's there. I'm convinced that we are better than conventional psychology has made us out to be."

Tom, meanwhile, was still acting as his therapist's therapist. "The prayer is *based* on serenity," he said. "The first half of it says to grant me the serenity to accept what I can't change. But then they throw in, 'Give me the courage to change what I can.' And then they add, ' . . . and the wisdom to know the difference.' "

Judy was weeping softly. "I think that I didn't know the difference," she said, her fingertips massaging her forehead.

"Is there something wrong with being comfortable?" he asked.

"I guess not. Maybe I was trying to change *my* discomfort, thinking that I knew what was better for you."

"If I change my comfortableness and my serenity, that would mean being uncomfortable. I don't want to do that. When people become uncomfortable . . . bad things could happen. What could happen?" he asked. "What could happen if I was not serene, not comfortable?"

"I don't know, but I should have asked a long time ago."

Exactly, I thought. I decided to interrupt. The paradox already had occurred. By entering his universe, I had disrupted the pattern, gotten Tom to tell me who he was rather than how he thought he should change. Paradoxically, he *had* changed. He had changed his perception of himself. Now I wanted him to take advantage of the opportunity to express to one of these pursuing women who he was and how he was *not* going to change, and maybe why. If he expressed it to Judy, I thought, it might serve as a model for how he might later express himself to his girlfriend.

Outside, I told Tom that I wanted him to cure her by teaching her to be serene. I told him that he was the expert, she his student. He returned to the chair and tried more or less unsuccessfully to continue. I interrupted him again and asked him to stand up and tell her why he deserved her appreciation.

Standing, he folded his arms and said, "How can I teach you to be serene? Don't take risks. If you never risk anything, you'll never be uncomfortable. Don't change anything. If you try to change things, that, too, can lead to discomfort. Don't try to change other people. Appreciate them as they are. Appreciate their qualities, and don't try to change them. If you try to change them—''

''I lose out,'' she said.

''You can lose out. You can lose serenity that way, by trying to change other people, by trying to control them. All role-playing aside, that I know to be true. Because I've tried to control and change people a lot in the past. And it gives me a lot of discomfort, a lot of—whatever the opposite was of serenity—whenever I tried to do that. But the key to that is knowing the difference. Knowing what you can change and what you can't.''

''I believe it,'' she said.

''Good.'' He paused, then smiled. ''Is it because I'm standing up?'' he asked gently.

''No,'' she said, looking up at him and smiling slightly herself.

I knocked again. ''I think you've done well,'' I told Tom. ''You can sit down.'' I walked to his chair and placed my right hand on his shoulder. ''I think that she probably needs another session with you. Probably one more. Would you agree?''

''I agree,'' he said.

''So, we'll stop for now. But you can see if you can fit her in your appointment book.''

''I'll have to see my secretary,'' he said.

We laughed, all three of us.

Judy later told me that she subsequently met several times with members of her family, particularly her father, and discussed his isolation and his withdrawal. He told her that he always had felt excluded by his wife and her family, with whom Judy had become very involved as daughter and granddaughter, and that after a while he had stopped risking feeling their rejection by just keeping to himself, especially around them. Following those conversations, Judy said, she eventually forgave her father.

Judy also told me that Tom had seen her for one more session, and that he and his girlfriend eventually had separated. I don't know what happened after that. But I thought about him often, and I incorporated that case into lectures about achieving failure.

Tom Martin had refashioned himself into a serene man in a heroic effort to change from alcohol-dependent to alcohol-independent. Was he to change again and become expressive in order to satisfy the needs of the women in his life? He was afraid to, but he felt obligated to, because he had accepted their perception of him as a withdrawn, noncommunicative, and therefore a failing personality. Once his perception changed, he first began to appreciate himself better, then became expressive enough to say that he wanted their appreciation but was not going to change to get it. That in itself represented a profound change, so Tom moved on and evidently left the others behind.

His "failure" in therapy with Judy Reed had protected his serenity. Judy's failure, meanwhile, gave her an opportunity to continue to attempt to repair her relationships with men in general, with her father and her husband specifically. Her stubborn persistence stemmed from an indefatigable optimism about fixing those old relationships, just as heroic, in a way, as Tom's steadfast refusal to yield to her notion of what should have been his behavior. In the wrong place, Judy's optimism served her purpose rather than Tom's therapy. In turning the tables, we provided the opportunity for the failure between them to become success. Tom articulated his serenity, ending Judy's failure, and then he rid himself of both women who refused to respect his success at achieving serenity. And Judy recognized and repaired her relationships with her men, so that she no longer needed to fail as Tom's therapist.

POSTSCRIPT

"Resistance" is a key word in therapy, and like all key words, it can be used—or abused—to blanket more truth than it reveals. For example: you are in therapy; you sense an impasse and decide that you want to quit the therapy. Your therapist, protecting himself, may then categorize your desire to quit as "resistance." That diminishes its significance, convinces you that you have created the impasse, and perpetuates the impasse under the guise of therapy for a resistant patient. The patient, out of respect for the therapist and his authority, may comply with the therapist's view by remaining in therapy but likely will also wisely hold on to his problem, having recognized that he is misunderstood by his therapist.

Frankly, it is often the therapist's resistance that results in an impasse—resistance to understanding the patient's dilemma or to recognizing the incorrectness of his own prescription, whether stated or covertly implied by his pattern of inquiries. Frequently, the therapist is following the rules of his own history as well as the rules of his profession. He reaches an impasse with his patient because part of the patient's pattern violates the therapist's allegiance to his own history. The therapist winds up trying to get the patient to change behavior that actually solves a problem, because that behavior reminds the therapist too well of a problem of his own. When the therapist does not understand the potential consequences of such a change, the patient develops a mechanism of refusal—appropriately so, though he doesn't know it—because subconsciously he does know that such change is fraught with consequences his therapist is not aware of or chooses to ignore.

The defensive therapist interprets this as the patient's resistance to therapy—as opposed to resistance to the therapist. This collection's title story, "The Patient Who Cured His Therapist," is a classic example of the problem. An impasse is perpetuated by a therapist who resists recognizing her own unresolved conflict, on the one hand, and the integrity of her patient, on the other.

In this case, it took a third party—me—to recognize and be able to analyze the situation, and to see how the therapist's attempted solution to the case was defeating everybody. (That alone struck me as ominous—and still does, whenever I ponder the implicit dangers of the artificial sanctity of the patient-therapist relationship. How wise are we, as patients, to entrust so subjective a science to the interpretive view of one practitioner, let alone to ensure, through a nearly sacramental secrecy, that his performance will go forever unexamined?)

At any rate, I intervened in the pattern of Tom Martin's therapy very early in the proceedings, by declaring him "serene," a positive quality, instead of the negative "withdrawn" or "resistant." I solidified the intervention by further suggesting that the women in his life did not understand his serenity. He was jarred by so respectful a characterization. I described him as content yet so generous at the same time that he would regularly see a therapist in order to soothe his girlfriend's discomfort with his contentedness; moreover, that he would remain in therapy for two solid years in order to salve the therapist's discomfort with this same pacific quality of his.

While he pondered this new and complimentary way of looking at himself, I further suggested that his therapist might be addicted to change and might be struggling, against his best interests, to serve her addiction by forcing him to change. So, the second intervention was to convince him that if he wanted this seemingly interminable therapy to end without his wanting to sacrifice his serenity, he might want to cure his therapist of her addiction to changing him.

Once I learned that he was a recovering alcohol addict, I was sure he could do it. He had on his hands an addictive person who had not come to terms with herself, could not sit still with her own anxiety about a man who was not communicative in a way that made her comfortable. She was compelled to change him to make herself more comfortable. She was resisting, refusing to understand the importance of the alcoholic's being the protector of his own serenity, because of her own addiction to change. I hoped I was using the moment between the therapist and the patient as a metaphor for their other relationships—patient and girlfriend, patient and mother, therapist and husband, therapist and father—so they might be able to transfer their discoveries to those relationships.

It was ironic for me, a therapist, to be taking a position that communicating openly and directly is not always the best course. It usually is, and in a society where communication is given the status of high art, "uncommunicative" men tend not to measure up to the standard. That may be true for many men, but the professional community must also recognize that many other men have good reasons for their own ways of communicating, however it may displease their more conventionally communicative partners. Again, we cannot judge behavior—silence, for instance—out of context.

THE WALL
OF SHEETS

New York, 1985

THE YOUNGEST OF SIX CHILDREN BY TEN YEARS, EAMONN Duly had left home on his twentieth birthday without leaving so much as a note or any attempt at an explanation. At first he could not say why, precisely. Fifteen years later, I saw in his face flashes of great, defiant pride in the boldness and lingering mystery of his departure. I also saw spasms of sadness.

My co-therapist and I at the Family Institute did not learn his history initially, which was unusual for us, and a mistake. He had grown up in Dromore, in Northern Ireland, a dreary market village, as he eventually described it, about fifteen miles south of Belfast. He attended Mass at the Dromore Cathedral, a Roman Catholic church in an area he described as punctuated by the pennants and the clubhouses of the dominant Protestant population. Union Jacks flapped from poles fastened to nearly every house outside of the immediate town, and an Orange Hall marked every third kilometer of winding roadway leading out of Dromore and into dairy farm areas with alternatingly lyrical and ominous names, like Tullymacarrett and Black Skull.

Eamonn described his childhood as bitterly harsh. His father, a non-practicing Catholic with almost tribal loyalties to the traditions of the have-nots hating the haves, was a brooding man, fearsome for his unpredictable bursts of binge drinking. Whenever the father failed to return from what servile tasks he could perform for surrounding land-owners and farmers, Eamonn's mother and even his older brothers lived in a bleak terror, counting the days of his absence. Ironically, they felt better the longer he was gone. If he ran out of money, he would be back in two days, drunk and angry enough to rage against his fate and healthy enough to wreak havoc on those with whom he shared it. If he did not return after three or four days, the family felt a pathetic relief, because he most assuredly would be sick or exhausted, or both.

Eamonn and his mother escaped to the church, though not together in spirit. Each sought institutional refuge; each considered the other incapable of protecting. In the church, the father's rejection metamorphosed into rigidity for the son. Eamonn seemed to have no tangible love for his religion, no sense of rapture, relief, or warmth when speaking about it. He was instead a soldier of Christ, he said. He abided by the rules. Conditions existed. His job was to live with them, not fight them. "What I do best is shrug?" he said with an interrogative lift to his final syllable, as if I was supposed to nod in agreement. All of his sentences ended that way. We had to retrain our ears for the unfamiliar ac-cent of Ulster. "I'm trudgin' hoam ta me wee hise? And whut does me skin feel behind me but the crasshairs of a scoop, ona backa me neck?" was not a pair of questions but declarative sentences designed to inaugurate a story about the brutality of British soldiers. We were forced to wrestle with the imagery of crosshairs and connect *scoop* to scope, while we still had not figured out that a *wee hise* was a small house. It took the better part of three sessions of marital therapy just to tune ourselves in to the rhythm and lyricism of the Dulys' language.

We learned. Later, we learned that Eamonn, feeling un-wanted and alienated from every institution except the church, had left school at sixteen and basically loitered about the central square in Dromore until he demanded of himself a commitment to one of two choices: fail or leave. He dressed himself one morning and "trudged" to the highway. He hitched a series of rides that landed him in Dublin a day later. There, by a coincidence that drove the frightened and sometimes superstitious young man to consult a priest, Eamonn encountered a reporter for *The Leader,* a newspaper with its main offices in the larger town of Banbridge and a satellite office near the square where Eamonn had spent so many of his aimless days. She recognized him on the street at random. She asked about his mother. She knew she had had a hard life, she said. Feeling every bit the traitor and the coward, Eamonn begged the reporter not to reveal his whereabouts to his mother. "O'm nuthin' but trubul fer me ma?" he said. "Hur prophecy fer me is prison, then hell. If she's even a wee accurate, I'll not break her heart twice by havin' her know the details. Please don't tell Ma ya seen me."

More than a dozen years later, he would only assume that the woman had complied.

Eamonn landed a job cleaning out a small restaurant and, through careful study and some deceit, passed himself off to another restaurateur as an experienced bartender. During a particularly busy period in the late 1970s, when young Irish restaurant workers were slipping quietly and illegally into the United States, Eamonn took a flight to New York to tend bar in an Irish tavern whose visiting Belfast-born proprietor he had served in Dublin. In Manhattan, he met Carmel Kane, a waitress whose voice he heard and loved for two days before he managed to catch a good glimpse of her. She approached him for drink orders via the service bar opening. She called it the "windy," which he recognized both as meaning "window" and as a familiar idiosyncrasy of provincial speech. He finally had to bend down, peer up, and ask where in the world, or in the North, she had learned to talk.

She was from Newry, so close to Dromore that Eamonn

could have walked there a hundred times, though he never had seen the place once in his life. But relatives of his mother's were from Newry, and in their initial conversations Carmel said she thought she had heard her own relatives mentioning his, somewhere, somehow.

The oldest of four, she always had excelled in school, where her sisters and brother had no patience for study. When she left home to seek her fortune in America, her two sisters were talking of quitting school and working for a pittance in a tiny Banbridge hotel. Her parents hoped that after a half decade or so of discovering America, Carmel would marry a rich man and send for them, or at least send them some money.

Carmel's green card expired three years later, and she was neither rich nor famous nor possessed of any status she could bring home to Ireland. By that time, too, she had met and taken refuge in Eamonn Duly, embracing his alienation as her shameful due. When they entered the Family Institute, she was the mother of three children and the wife of a man with whom she fought incessantly and often cruelly, trading eloquent sarcasm that cut deeply into their shared secrets. Still, they were resolute in their determination to keep their family together and their marriage intact. Separation was not an alternative. Eamonn said up front that he had been an alcoholic, but alcoholism was less a theme than we might first have expected, given his past and the history of both of them working in an atmosphere of consumption and addiction. Eamonn said that he hadn't taken a drink in almost two years, and Carmel nodded affirmatively. She said that his drinking had added to their difficulties, but that their disagreements actually had become more severe since he had stopped.

I and my co-therapist, Alice Tripp, saw the Dulys in the context of a couple's therapy group. We were using a technique Peggy Papp had developed and called Couples Choreography. Basically, this involved the participants' projecting metaphoric descriptions of the problem in their relationship in a nearly cinematic way, using animals, objects, shapes, natural phenomena—anything other than themselves—to describe their perception, their behavior, and the dynamic of their interaction in the relationship. Couples were asked to act out or choreograph the relationship using these metaphors. Without the language most familiar to them, they were forced to describe their complex relationships in images Peggy liked to describe as "uncensored by logic." Typically, we used the choreography technique in the first session to help define the couple's perception of their relationship and then throughout the therapy as a measure of assessing change.

In dealing with the other couples in the group, our experiences were fascinating, enlightening, and fruitful. With the Dulys, the early sessions especially were completely uninteresting, and our progress ranged from slow to nonexistent. Other couples participated in their own therapy, whereas the Dulys resisted. For instance, we asked all the couples to close their eyes and conjure a fantasy about the problem or the dilemma in their relationship, to think about their relationship in a symbolic form parallel, say, to the way we dream. What form, what object or animal or other person would they and their partner appear as in such a dream? Could they bring these forms or objects together in a way that symbolically expressed the nature of the problem in the relationship?

One woman imagined that her husband was an elephant and that she was a parasite feeding off the elephant's back. She could not live unless she fed off the elephant's back, but she understood that the elephant also was dependent on parasites to clean him, as in the symbiosis of the jungle. The fantasy reflected the mirror image of the husband's presenting complaint, that she constantly was trying to reform him, shape him up, change him. In his fantasy, she was a hen, hungry and demanding, and he a fat green worm, soft on the outside, hard on the inside. He feared that if he softened on the inside, he would become delectable, and the hen would devour him.

Both fantasies expressed the extreme dependency, both expressed the idea of feeding off one another. The beauty of the technique was that it got to the heart of the problem almost immediately. Symbols and metaphors presented a visible description of what was going on, and the therapy proceeded from the picture. As the therapy took its course, the couple would reveal different dreams about different issues, but this first one articulated the reason they sought therapy. From there we moved on to another technique called Family Sculpting, wherein we asked people to physically position the members of their family in a way that would reflect the structure of relationships, the alliances and the distances between members. Later, we would ask for dreams about their families of origin, about their hopes for the future. As the therapy progressed, the techniques revealed information and indicated the progress of the couple.

In the case of the Dulys, we saw no progress.

In Carmel Duly's first fantasy, she presented herself as a cat, Eamonn as a dog. She said she had changed from a timid to a snarling cat over the years to protect herself from her husband. However, not liking herself as a snarling cat, she then became the kind of timid cat who slinked away from the attacks, as a way of maintaining some control of the situation.

Eamonn said his mind was blank. He could not have such a fantasy. In discussing hers, though, he at least revealed his basic pessimism about their relationship. He said cats and dogs were natural born enemies who never could get along. He seemed to see himself as withdrawing from her in an attempt to avoid conflict. And actually, that was true, though we did not see it clearly at the time. As a team, we were not performing well at all, and I think we knew it clinically even as we sensed it instinctively.

Carmel and Eamonn alternated between attacking and

withdrawing, each taking the opposite position in each battle. They seemed to see each other as enemies most of the time, yet they continued to insist that they belonged together. We, the therapists, continued not to "get it." We continued to focus on the surface appearance of their failure and not on its function, and so we continued to fail ourselves.

We asked them to spend an evening alone together, without the three children, with whom they both were heavily involved, probably as another means of avoiding each other. We described it as a pre-test, like a spelling test that doesn't count, or a pre-season game, a straightforward attempt to see if their difficulties were changeable. If so, we would encourage change as part of the pre-test, and in an attempt to get them to pay attention to each other, we asked them to monitor each other's experiences. They agreed, but they said at the next session that they did not take the pre-test. Eamonn had worked an unexpected double shift on the day they had set aside for it, and Carmel was busy with the children, anyway. Ultimately, they admitted that they both were afraid to place much hope in their relationship, for fear of being let down when the hope was shattered. We assumed from their failure even to try the pre-test that they were not yet ready to make any changes for themselves. We assumed furthermore that they needed to make changes.

In another session, Eamonn said he had managed to imagine a fantasy to tell us. He saw himself as a porpoise swimming alone in the ocean, completely and blissfully free. When we asked where Carmel might fit into this scene, since the fantasy was supposed to be about their relationship, he seemed surprised. He said flatly that if Carmel were in the fantasy, he could not be the porpoise. Next, Carmel had a fantasy in which she described them as two people walking as if on eggs, to avoid bumping into each other, as if any contact between them were risky.

We understood from their fantasies that they were deeply anxious about the possibility of connectedness. They distanced themselves from each other either by fighting or avoidance. If they weren't battling, they were retreating. Eamonn offered yet another image that excluded Carmel, that he was a horse, galloping across green fields and over stone fences, returning to his home stable. As he approached the stable, however, his eyes bulged, his breath shortened, and his pulse quickened with the fear of entrapment. He turned abruptly and charged off.

So, with the idea that at some level the distance between them was important, that if they were closer, Eamonn would feel he was losing his freedom, we told them to try to maintain the distance and not get too close. Still trying to get them to change, though, we offered a prescription for separating, both to honor their distance and to soothe the pain it caused. "It is going to sound strange to you," Alice said, "and you will understand it only as you do it, but we feel that the strong current of your hostility may be the bond that keeps you close. We want you to try, every time you separate—when, for example, you leave to go to work—to ritualize the separation with a good-bye kiss. Whenever you feel hostile, we would also like you to try to punctuate your hostility with a kiss, so that the kiss is used to designate your distance and separation, not your closeness and affection."

They were able to follow through on this ritual, and they did say that friendlier feelings began to emerge as a result, but it was a fundamentally contradictory prescription. During that time Carmel began to make attempts to get closer to Eamonn, and he responded by intensifying his involvement in whatever activities kept him away from her, including but not limited to becoming hostile. Carmel said she now saw herself as a frightened little dog seeking warmth and companionship from her master, who constantly pushed her away. Her efforts made it look on the surface as if one partner was making progress at least, but since the other partner reacted in a diametrically opposite way, the overall effect was the same distance. The tenacity of a pattern like that almost always suggests complicity.

Alice and I became acutely aware that whatever we were doing, it was not working. We reviewed the tapes again and again. Were we being too strategic? Perhaps we were approaching the problem without a deep enough understanding of the couples' past histories. Perhaps we needed more on their backgrounds.

We asked them to tell us their autobiographies. Eamonn wove his sad tale, weeping when he related his conversation in Dublin with the reporter from *The Leader.* He said he was a difficult son, a lout and a layabout. He described himself as a double failure—he could not summon the courage to protect his mother in the first instance, and then he abandoned her. She was right about him, he said. Though he adhered to the rules, he still should wind up in prison, then in hell.

Carmel sobbed openly when she talked about leaving her family, particularly her mother. Her childhood had been close to idyllic, except for the periodic responsibilities she had had for her younger sisters and brother. Her father, though distant, was kind. Her mother was an angel. "She wanted so much fer me?" Carmel cried. "Ya know I didn't live up."

Carmel's parents were supposed to have visited New York several years after the Dulys were married. It would have been their first trip to the United States—their first flight, for that matter—and Carmel's eager anticipation was so palpable, Eamonn agreed, that even he got caught up in the excitement. The visit would be lengthy, six weeks at least, and Carmel planned to show, escort, or direct them to all that was wonderful in New York and the environs. Two weeks before they were to have arrived, Carmel's father telephoned to say that her mother was quite ill, seriously enough so that not only was the trip cancelled, but Carmel might also consider making a trip home, just in case it turned out to be a last visit.

Despite the Dulys' shaky financial situation, both agreed that Carmel should make the trip. During the flight, and unbeknownst to Carmel, her mother died. Carmel arrived in time for a wake and a funeral. Her remorse was bottomless. She had left her mother to achieve and return triumphant. She had not achieved and had returned a mourner.

During this time, Eamonn added, he was plagued with thoughts of his own mother and seriously considered writing her a letter of deep and profound apology. But he did not. And when Carmel returned from Ireland, the problems between them increased almost exponentially.

We interrupted that autobiographical session for a discussion between me and Alice and resumed it with another intervention, which amounted to yet another attempt to change them. We said because they both suffered such pain and remorse about having abandoned their mothers, that in the tradition of both their families and their religion, it might be useful for them to do some penance, to help them ultimately absolve themselves of guilt. Furthermore, we said, we had thought about this and determined that the penance ought to be severe. Our suggested penance for them was that they sit down and communicate with each other in at least a civil fashion and on a regular basis. Eamonn smiled a broad Irish grin that reminded me of the actor Brian Dennehy, who frequently broke into a smile, accompanied by a head movement that always left me wondering whether the smile said, "I see what you mean. You're right," or "You still don't get it, stupid. You may never get it."

Between that session and the next, Alice and I reviewed all the tapes again and discussed the case at length and very self-critically. We theorized that our continuing efforts to change the Dulys grew out of our own needs, not theirs. Somehow their needs were being fulfilled by their adherence to their pattern, as if they were best served by having an invisible wall between them, to keep them from what we would have judged to be a successful relationship. Maybe theirs was a successful relationship for their mutual needs.

But why would that be so?

The idea jumped out at both of us simultaneously: the very distance we were trying to help them bridge was in fact a wall that they had raised, through silence or anger or both, which we suddenly saw as constructed with the bricks and mortar of family loyalty. As long as Eamonn perceived himself as an imprisoned traitor, a failed son, he at least was being loyal to his mother's judgment. Were he to have run away and become blissfully successful in every life endeavor, he would have finalized his betrayal and even rejoiced in it, which was against his every conditioned instinct. He would be proving his mother wrong about him, declaring definitively that his running away was fruitful and productive and made him happy, and he couldn't bring himself to do it. Carmel, on the other hand, saw herself as having let her family down, marrying an alcoholic bartender, and could not then justify being happy to have done it. She already was doing penance. She owed her mother at least some misery in her contrition. For each of them, the final, dreaded abandonment of their mothers would be the bond of a successful marriage.

Having recognized this, we returned to them in the next session and said that we finally understood the profound value of the distance between them, which they cleverly maintained through a delicate combination of combat and withdrawal, confrontation and avoidance. Their behavior had created a wall. At some level it was a wall of misery, but it was also a functional wall, which served to keep them from finally and definitively betraying their families. We said we had talked it over and had decided to ask them to build a real wall, in their home, to remind them that the distance between them was both functional and not to be breached.

"Neither of you has been able to forgive yourselves for having abandoned your families," Peggy told them. "The wall you have built between each other is actually an act of loyalty to them. In a way, it is a holy wall, giving you a spiritual connectedness to the families you both left behind.

We think you should bless it, thank God for it, make it real.''

I said, ''You may never be able to communicate, or expect to communicate, the way other people are expected to do. Perhaps the best you can do is to bless your wall, be thankful for it, accept it, and maybe the harm will then go out of it.'' We further suggested that they make the wall out of sheets, because sheets were inexpensive, penetrable, more symbolic than real, and could be dismantled for such practical considerations as social gatherings with friends who would neither understand nor deserve an explanation.

We saw the Dulys for two more sessions. In the first, Eamonn reported that they had not built the wall of sheets, that he felt uneasy about its seeming artifice. However, he arrived looking different. He had shaved his beard. He was dressed more nattily, and he said that he and Carmel were planning a trip home to Ireland. They had attended Mass together for the first time in a long while, and they both had talked much more freely and analytically about their relationships with their families and their pain and guilt about having left them. In the last session, Eamonn spoke openly and even grandly of his acceptance of the idea of the wall, and the fact that he had erected it in their Upper West Side apartment. Furthermore, he said, he sensed that the harm from their fighting had diminished considerably for their having accepted the function it served. He no longer was fighting fighting, he said, but was engaging in it as a necessary and protective choreography. Carmel agreed. The animosity had disappeared from their disagreements. The sarcasm was more playful than painful. They found each other grinning in the smoky aftermath of a battle. They said the wall had given their lives a certain clarity that either had not existed before or that they had not seen before.

It almost seems too neat an ending, but I happen to live on the Upper West Side, and a year later, I really did see Eamonn Duly in a store. He was leaving as I was entering, and he caught my look of recognition, although I did not know right away why he looked so familiar to me. He was carrying a stack of new sheets, and the sight of them rang a chord in my memory. He looked at me, startled at first, then sheepish. He hefted the sheets slightly and said his next stop was the rectory of his parish church, where he would ask the priest to bless the sheets.

I smiled and nodded, then shook his hand.

POSTSCRIPT

In this case, I was guilty of failing to see what I had long preached: that what appeared to be problematic behavior in a relationship was actually a solution to a problem. Also, my co-therapist and I had reached an impasse with a couple because we were stuck, not they. We were unable or unwilling to grasp the poetic meaning of their conflict as their own adaptive way of reconciling each other's opposing loyalties. We insisted, instead—to the couple, to each other, and to ourselves—that the couple had to change their behavior in order to stabilize their relationship. For the longest time, we refused to see that their behavior already had stabilized their relationship. For example, our idea of the parting kiss was a paradoxical prescription intended to promote change. We were getting desperate by that point, trying anything—still refusing to acknowledge that their separateness was their solution. The prescription had a certain logic, a symbol of closeness acting as a touchstone of the couple's distance; in retrospect, it shows that we at least had realized that the distance between them was very important. But, stuck to a vague idea predicated on the push for change, we had not yet admitted that their distance was their destination, not their direction.

The couple taught us, finally, by their steadfast refusal to change that they were determined to maintain their own method of reconciliation. They were not resisting us; we were resisting them. We were acting on our own ambitions to do what we had been programmed to do—make people change in order to feel better. Finally, we recognized that we could not help them by changing such reconciliations as they had made. We could help make them less painful by giving due respect to their traditions and by helping them symbolize the function of their separateness so that their separateness would become more obvious, accepted, and detoxified, even sanctified.

To my surprise, recognizing our mistake came as a great joy and a relief to me. I did not feel foolish for behaving as if I had not heard my own lectures, or arrogant for stubbornly insisting that my education and experience gave me a better knowledge of the Dulys' relationship than they had. I had felt downright disrespectful about continually trying to move them in one or another direction of our invention. I should have paid that feeling greater heed earlier, examined it more closely. After all the frustration, recognizing this mistaken approach really punctuated for me my own oft-stated point: pushing for or encouraging change can be a personal-professional hindrance to therapy, when the best course might be merely to identify the dilemmas and the potential consequences of each alternative solution at a given moment.

TRANSCENDING
ILLUSIONS

∎

Illusions, subconscious spasms of creativity, arise from a desperate need to transform the details of reality and make them more pleasant, satisfying, exciting, or challenging than their creator considers them at the moment. People organize illusions to help them deal with acute or serious anxiety caused by situations or circumstances, as a mother of four does with the help of the *Reader's Digest* in the story entitled "Sin's Syndrome." Sometimes the illusion passes with the crisis, but sometimes, as in the mother's case, it becomes fixed over time because it functions to balance an attempt to reconcile the past and future, or to postpone a confrontation between past deeds and future consequences, mainly by avoiding the unpleasant details of the reality.

In "Father Knows Best," one member of the family in the service of another, and with the assistance of still other family members in a collaborative effort, assumes a burden of tremendous anxiety in order to love and protect the more hurting member. All of them believe that the hurting family member is not yet able to handle her problem. The illusion that the strong member is fraught with anxiety gives the weak one both the protection she requires and whatever time she needs to prepare to face her own worst fears.

The two "Spaghetti Stories" suggest that some illusions become sacred and permanent in themselves, and for reasons that will forever remain a mystery; while others drift in and out of accepted reality as the need arises for them, and require only better management. Like failures, illusions work, perform a function, achieve a goal. The therapist's challenge is to discover the purpose of the illusion and define it, perhaps to appreciate it when he cannot.

THE TWO
SPAGHETTI
STORIES

New York, 1974

1

AT THE BEGINNING AND THE END OF THE FIRST YEAR OF MY
training, I encountered two patients, Florence and Grace,
each of whom had created a separate reality for herself that
challenged my own and raised questions about the very nature of what reality was.

I met Florence first, at a dreary clinic on the grounds of
an even drearier state-operated psychiatric hospital. I was
the equivalent of an intern, working under the supervision
of professionals who were as dedicated to the traditional
psychoanalytical approach to the behavioral studies as I was
sorely tempted, but not yet ready, to rebel from it.

I was young. I had a plan to change the world, and I was
eager to get started, knowing, as I did, that the work was
going to take months at the very least.

I spotted Florence at an orientation briefing. I and my
student colleagues were invited to shuffle into a small,
musty gymnasium, whose brown-painted heating pipes
seemed to be kicking each other awake whenever the oil
burner yawned to life, sounding as if someone in a nearby
anteroom were tuning the radiators with a nightstick. Moments after we gathered at mid-court, a handful of obviously skeptical attendants herded in a mini-busload of
patients so forlorn in their appearance that I'm certain sev-

eral of us immediately flirted in our imaginations with the notion of alternative vocations, like driving a cab, or cleaning graffiti off subway trains.

Our job, and the patients' job, was to select each other, quite randomly, as potential partners in education and therapy. By mingling with them, we might get an idea of just how difficult and/or challenging this work might be. By mingling with us, each of them might finally encounter the one unjaded, undefeated genius who could answer such prayers as they might have been praying had they been administered lesser dosages of medication.

Florence was last to enter the room, seconds after an observant and, I guess, kind attendant had told me she would be. He said she always was last, as she was also the last to leave the bus, or to enter it, or to queue up to eat, or to sit down to string beads.

She wore a nondescript housedress with a pale argyle sweater draped over her shoulders. Some synthetic hormonal ingredient in her daily medication had seeded her upper lip with a spare but unattractively dark mustache, which she apparently never considered removing or bleaching. She wore yellow terrycloth slippers and sweat socks whose elastic had grown as fatigued and apathetic as the hands that declined to pull them up.

Florence carried a Styrofoam cup of coffee in one hand and a lit cigarette in the other, always. Frank, the attendant, told me that she chain-smoked—literally. He had never seen her touch a match to the end of a cigarette and guessed that she required only one match each day, obviously first thing in the morning. He correctly predicted her every move, up to and including the move that rendered her thereafter motionless. He said she would shuffle over to a seat next to the piano bench, and she did. He said she would then stare straight ahead, and she did that. He said she would not flick but more or less allow her cigarette ashes to fall off, forming a little gray island around her, and she did that. When anyone needed access to the piano, he said, one or two of the attendants would lift Florence, chair and all, and move her aside, and she would not flinch during portage. By that time I had no reason to doubt Frank's word. Finally, he said that she would not talk to anyone, not ever, that she never had, and that if I thought for a moment that I could get through to her, I would be wasting my time. I glanced at Frank as the question "What makes you say that?" crossed my mind, and he answered it before I got the chance to edit my thoughts.

"You have that look," he said.

I had to laugh.

"I get the feeling that you've seen student therapists once or twice before," I said.

He had to laugh.

But he was right. I already was tempted to begin changing the world by introducing its promise to Florence. She was irresistible. Her withdrawal created a gravitational pull that seemed directed right at me.

Her history: she was in her mid-thirties, though she looked fifteen years older. Born into a psychiatric ward, the daughter of a full-time patient and a part-time rapist, Florence had grown to junior high school age in three different foster homes, and upon reaching puberty she was diagnosed—or maybe denounced, I thought—as "catatonic hebephrenic," severely regressed, hallucinatory, and "deluded" by life.

I watched her intently for what seemed like (but was not) fifteen minutes or so, when I thought I noticed her lips, then her head, move forward and back ever so slightly. Why, she was conducting a conversation! All right, maybe only half a conversation. Her counterpart in the discussion may well have been hallucinatory, but she was clearly talking. Already I had made a discovery that had gone undetected by the rest of the profession.

"I thought you said she didn't talk," I whispered excitedly to Frank. "Look at her now. Look at her!"

"No," Frank said without looking up. "Listen to her. Slide over there quietly and listen to her."

I walked nearer. She stopped, *I* thought because of my approach. But then she sipped her coffee, puffed on her cigarette, and resumed the monologue. I drew closer. She stared ahead, talking. Finally I was within earshot. I strained to hear what she was saying. When I heard it, I strained harder to decipher it.

"Stallbig. Fraymore ball duff mon ling doo. Desimore. Banadore lymink shraboleen. Dorf."

Not one of her phonetic concoctions amounted to a word, not even mistakenly. She had created a language specific to her isolation, and so specifically *for* her isolation that she had assiduously avoided even an accidental swipe at any combination of vowel and consonants someone else might understand. I listened for more, and I got more. It was remarkable. She could talk paragraphs of what anybody else would consider nonsense syllables. I didn't think there could be that many nonsense syllables.

I pulled up a chair in front of her and sat down, facing her. I said, "Hello, Florence. I'm Stanley Siegel, an intern here. It's nice to meet you."

She stopped talking, or whatever it was she had been doing with her sounds. I was encouraged by the cessation and continued my conversation. She stared straight ahead, occasionally sipping, occasionally puffing.

"I've only been here a short time," I said. "I'm not at all familiar with the place, although I bet you are. Perhaps one of these days you could show me around. I mean, if you want, if it would be all right with you." She stared ahead. I talked on, complimenting her sweater and yellow slippers, avoiding looking at her mustache, making small talk about the weather, droning on insufferably, I suppose, until I began to suspect that she was patiently ignoring me, waiting for me to stop, or to finish, or to grow old and die. After a while I thanked her for her time. I rose and walked away, whereupon she sipped and puffed and resumed her syllables.

I repeated the exercise every day for weeks, conducting one-sided conversations in English, wherein I reported to her as much news as I could remember about the other patients and the staff and the bus drivers and the weather and whatever entered my mind. She stared ahead, sipping and puffing. Whenever I finished, she launched into her phonetic mysteries.

What a wonder she was, I thought. If her life was so awful, had she not managed to create a private, peaceful, and presumably interesting life inside her imagination and outside the institution, outside all institutions, even the institution of language?

At first I stubbornly determined to wear her down with my kindness. For years afterward, I thought of my efforts as wasted time, but I no longer feel that way. I learned a great deal from the weeks and weeks I spent trying to talk Florence into talking to me. At the time, however, I got absolutely nowhere.

I talked to her, or at her, for thirty minutes each day, and the entire time she stared ahead, puffing and sipping, puffing and sipping. I read newspaper stories to her. I told her about the traffic outside the hospitals in the morning and in the evening. I recited sports scores to her and tried to incite a reaction by insulting otherwise sacrosanct heroes of American baseball, football, basketball, and Olympic teams. I talked of recipes, painting schemes, party favors, wedding gifts, automobile styles, weather patterns, fabric preferences, contemporary decor, architecture, the comparative characteristics of different woods, the mysterious lives of eccentric artists, the intellectual difficulties presented by organized religions, the miasma of global politics, and the infuriating qualities of various inventions designed to hang a heavy painting on a plaster wall.

Nothing. No reaction. Sip and puff. Sip and puff.

One night I awoke with what I thought was an original

idea, a potential key. Later, I learned it and used it as a tactic. I also learned that it was not an original idea at all, and that I probably had heard or read of it before, under the category of "joining" a patient's "universe." But in the middle of the night, during a period of protracted frustration, it felt like a world-altering discovery, and I remember the joy it brought me the way old men remember the joys of Christmas mornings when they still believed in Santa Claus.

I would talk to Florence in her language. I would join her. I would invent nonsense syllables similar to hers. If they meant nothing, she would hear the same nonsense she heard when I spoke English to her. If I stumbled onto sounds that she understood, she might recognize me and try to reciprocate. If she was really talking nonsense syllables as a device for escaping, my joining her might cause her to see the futility and downright silliness of her tactic, and she would recognize it and talk to me.

God, I hope nobody eavesdropped on my one-sided conversations.

"Brendeel wain bathenloom," I said as Florence stared ahead, making no eye contact, sipping and puffing, waiting for me to finish. "Lornell foppin dooz. Manya frandish. Via mastindike sheem. Drolin thab rol mickindelle fut mandaloon. Ord? Foy maindee! Rame dell stadlerbem char davenborg . . ."

I did that for another week at least, for a half hour every day.

Once she interrupted me and barked a syllable I thought I recognized as one of my own inventions. She continued staring straight ahead, sipping and puffing, but I convinced myself that I had seen the flicker of a major breakthrough. I was encouraged in a fashion so exaggerated, I felt compelled to continue babbling to Florence for a daily half hour right up to the last morning of my internship.

About a week before the year's end, I was working at a desk in an office I borrowed from nine to ten every morning, mainly to fill out admission and insurance forms and coordinate appointments. Someone knocked on the door. I had told those patients considered mine that I would be borrowing that office for the same hours every day, should they ever feel the need to talk on days that we did not have a formal appointment. I did have patients other than Florence, and I did experience some success with them. But as the year's end grew nearer, I felt increasing frustration about only one patient, my dear, intractable Florence, who, as I opened the office door, appeared before me, holding her ever present props in either hand.

"Florence!" I exclaimed.

She sipped her coffee.

"Florence, come in, please. How nice to see you! Have a seat."

"I have something on my mind," she said, staring past me, then puffing on her cigarette.

I could barely hold myself together. She spoke! I think my heart rate set off alarms in another part of the hospital. For all I knew, it was the first English-language sentence Florence had said to anyone in years. I had broken through! Florence was going to talk to me, perhaps even rejoin my world after years in her own. Which was the key? Did she trust me because of my patience? Was it that I had joined her in the nonsense syllables? Had I shown her the respect that she deserved for creating her own functioning, private universe, or had I revealed to her the frivolity of her linguistic escape? Where were the doubting Thomases now? Where were my supervisors? Where was the media? I thought I would burst.

"Florence!" I stammered. "Something on your mind! Well, please, come in. Come in! On your mind. Of course, on your mind. What else would it be on? Tell me. What's on your mind, Florence? Yes, yes. What *is* on your mind? *What* is on your mind?"

And she answered:

"Spaghetti."

"Spaghetti," I repeated.

Spaghetti was on her mind. Staring straight ahead, past my right ear, Florence sipped her coffee and took a short, hasty drag on her cigarette. She was done telling me what was on her mind. I had asked. She had answered: spaghetti.

But she *had* come to me, had she not? She had knocked on my door, and during the appointed hour. She had said a declarative sentence in English: "I have something on my mind." And then I had asked what. And she had told me.

She turned around in three shuffling steps and walked away. She resumed her station in the chair nearest the piano. She resumed her staring. She resumed her sipping and puffing. She resumed her syllabic symphony, leaving me to ponder the eternal mysteries of spaghetti and, now and then, to laugh at myself.

The reasons for her constructing this reality were inaccessible now, long in the past, and probably irrelevant. This new reality existed with as much validity and solidity as my own did, I thought, with its own language, ritual, and comforts. Here I was thinking that our reality was the better one or the right one, or that she had no control over her illusion, but in fact she proved to be a master of it, in absolute control. She showed me that her reality was sacred, my meddling blasphemous. Eventually I thought of her case as a lesson rather than a failure, and applied what she taught me. With another case—the next story—I built on the idea, not only respecting the patient's illusions, but joining them and making them my own.

2

During the same intern year that I endured my humbling experience with Florence, I also began seeing Grace, who was then approaching fifty years of age. Unintentionally unemployed for the tenth or eleventh time, Grace had been a patient under every possible circumstance in a number of psychiatric institutions over the previous ten years. She had been admitted; she had admitted herself. She had been recommended, remanded, required, and even sentenced to hospital stays. She represented quite a challenge for a beginning therapist.

Again, under the tutelage and influence of a disciple of the traditional psychoanalytic approach, I was getting nowhere, and as the year wore inexorably on, my estimation of my progress with Grace, and my concomitant frustration, threatened to rival her depression over her own apparent difficulties.

From the window of the clinic, I watched once a week as Grace parked her car in the metered lot across the street. She would get out of the car and scrutinize the distance between its wheels and the white lines bordering the space. She then would gauge the distance between the front right wheel and the line nearest it, and compare that with the distance between the rear right wheel and the same line. If the distances did not match to her satisfaction, Grace would get back into the car, put it in gear, and correct whatever she had determined to be the inexactitude. Then she would get out and review the relative distances again.

When she was satisfied on the right side, she would begin the process anew on the left, each time readjusting the measurements by moving the car, and therefore always spoiling the first measurements and risking having to start all over again.

Finally she would compare the distance between the fenders of the car and the respective white lines on either side, making sure that the car was properly centered and perfectly parallel to the borders of the parking space.

The process often took a half hour or more, and in order to both endure and enjoy it, I adapted my schedule to accommodate Grace's early arrival. I made her my first appointment of the day, or my first appoint after an hour break, so I could watch Grace without robbing another patient of my attentions; and so I could ponder as well my changing approach to her, usually with an eye toward re-directing it according to the ever changing theories that were maturing in my mind.

Grace nurtured a rather flattering view of herself in rela-tionship to the world around her. When she finally arrived at my office, she would immediately launch into extended, uninterruptible, and sometimes mysteriously cogent expla-nations of how and why she was directly responsible for the Vietnam War, the extended drought in the Sahara, the endangered-species status of the North Atlantic osprey, and the failure of manufacturers of the Mazda automobile to successfully market the Wankel, a rotary combustion en-gine. Needless to say, these treatises were as fascinating as any I had heard or read in my lifetime. If my job was to understand their origins or "cure" Grace of her propensity to conjure them, however, I was a mighty failure at it.

After two years of analytic struggle, I began to "join" her delusions, slightly after the fashion of my "joining" Flor-ence's linguistic fantasies, but not in so radical a way as to appear as daft myself. I decided that if Grace's fantasies fascinated me, I would tell her so, and then probe with her what seemed to me so remarkable about them. When she repeated therefore that she had single-handedly started the war in Southeast Asia, I said, in as genuine a tone of awe as I could manage, that in my pathetic ignorance, I had not known of her titanic responsibility and never would have guessed it. Then I asked her to tell me specifically how she had started the war and what she hoped to gain by keeping it going. I exhibited passionate curiosity about every detail. I also produced examples of current literature on Vietnam and asked her to show me where it was wrong and where her name should have appeared.

I sensed that the tactic was starting to work when she began to laugh at the absurdity of some of my questions, and later at my notions. I told her at one point that I had been so appalled by the manner in which the U.S. military had minimized her contribution to the war effort that I had considered writing a letter on her behalf to General William C. Westmoreland. I said that friends of mine had served as officers on his public information staff in Saigon, and that through them my influence might force Westmoreland and the rest of officialdom to right the wrongs they had done her and set the record straight. The more specific I became, the more reality I began to interject into her fantasy, the clearer it became to her that my continued participation in her fantasies was becoming ridiculous. Following that, her fantasies were beginning to become ridiculous for her to hear. Once I entered and eventually took over her fantasy world, robbing her of its exclusivity, I forced her to consider surrendering it. After all, she didn't feel so much of a need for it anymore.

After another few months, we were chatting and laughing about the imagination she had exhibited in constructing the fantasies, as if we were therapists together reviewing an old case. Then she would spend the better part of a session telling how she had found herself wandering in one of the fantasies, how she had thought about the fantasy in terms of our conversations, how she had imagined and even created similar conversations by herself, and how she then laughed herself out of her own fantasies in the same way we had done together in the consultation room.

Consequently, she was able to abandon the fantasies more rapidly. Not that she didn't have them anymore. She did. But she gave them up more quickly. She didn't wander around in them anymore; she got out.

With all the free time and energy she now had, she was able to concentrate more on the other elements of her life. She could even hold a job. She enrolled in a hairdressing academy, attended regularly for the required weeks, and started a new career as a hairdresser. She developed a following and was satisfied with herself for the first time in many years.

Grace still was a fragile person, of course, and she called me at least once a year for ten years, alternately just to check in, to report how she felt, to make sure I was still alive and available for consultation, and now and then to permit herself the luxury of a relapse into an exaggerated reality.

One year she called in what sounded over the telephone like a perfect mixture of panic and euphoria, and I learned in the first half minute of her rapid-fire rambling that it was just that. She had, after years and years of preoccupation with herself, entered into somewhat of a relationship with a man, Bob, whose hair she had been cutting for six years and whose wife had died within the past six months.

I congratulated her and asked some perfectly innocuous question like, "Is he nice?" She did not appear to hear the question as she chattered on.

"It's going well. It's going well," she said. "Imagine that. Me. I'm dating a man, and it's going well, and I'm cooking him dinner. Right now. Here, in my own apartment. I decided to cook spaghetti. He likes pasta. At least I think he likes pasta. He said pasta is good for you. He worries about the fat content in meat and the cholesterol content in other things, and too much salt here, too little fiber there. But he says that pasta is very good, and I like pasta, and I'm making spaghetti."

"Grace!" I said. "That's wonderful. That's very nice—"

"No. Not yet, it's not. I mean, it could be very nice. But I'm making the sauce, you see. And I decided to make it an authentic Italian sort of sauce: spicy. Fra diavolo. I think that means, 'brother of the Devil,' don't you know; or, 'Father Devil,' although that would be absurd, wouldn't it? *Father* Devil? You might as well say Reverend Devil or Rabbi Devil. The Most Holy Unholy Devil. Ha!

"But it means hot, whatever it is. Hot, obviously, as hell. When it's applied to a spaghetti sauce, you see, theology has no bearing on it. We're talking eternal flames. It means the sauce is hot. My problem is, what if it's too hot? What if I make the sauce and he can't stand it, because it's so hot? And then, of course, he'll eat it, because he's such a good man. Polite. Doesn't want to insult me. And then, of course, he gets sick, because of my fra diavolo sauce. If that happens, I've ruined the entire thing, haven't I? I've single-handedly cooked the first comforting relationship I might have had in fifteen years. Twenty years. Could it be twenty years? My God, Stanley! I won't be able to stand it. I can't take the responsibility of cooking sauce. Don't you see? Look at the metaphor here. Basically, I can cook my own goose right now, today. Stan, listen to me! What if the sauce is so hot, Bob eats the spaghetti and has a heart attack? What if I kill him with spaghetti?''

"Grace," I interrupted. "I have a great idea! Listen to me. Really. Just listen for a minute."

"I'm listening."

"Use my recipe for sauce. I have a recipe."

"You do?"

"Well, sort of. It's not a fra diavolo sauce. I mean, it's not hot. You can't get a heart attack from it."

"Oh, that's good. What's in it?"

"Hold on one second, I'll get it." I ran to the pantry and grabbed an armload of small bottles from the spice shelf. I also eyeballed every benign label I could see in there, hoping to be able to memorize some of the names. I returned to the phone and told her to begin with extract of vanilla, mixing it with a can of tomato sauce and a can of cream of mushroom soup, more or less to soften the spicy edge of the tomato sauce. I recommended adding a tablespoon of brown sugar and some sesame seed oil.

"Wait," she said. "Maybe I should write . . . Stanley!" she exclaimed. "Extract of vanilla? In a spaghetti sauce?''

"It sweetens the sauce."

"Whoever heard of a sweet spaghetti sauce?''

"I also put in applesauce and sour cream, to help coat the stomach lining."

"Stanley!"

"And a special garnée I make, by pulverizing an Alka-Seltzer tablet and sprinkling it over each individual serving of spaghetti—''

"You are *impossible*! You're doing it to me again, aren't you! I slipped, didn't I? Of course I did. Well, you bastard, thank you."

I must say, I felt pretty smug. This time, however, I knew I was feeling pretty smug, and I entertained no guilt whatsoever about my smugness, because I felt secure that I had deserved it. I made myself some soup. I made a pitcher of iced tea. I settled into my favorite chair with my favorite book, and I read until I could no longer hold my head upright. I really enjoyed myself. I retired that night feeling like a surgeon who had arrived on the scene of an accident at just the right moment.

The telephone answering machine blurted out my own voice at two-thirty or three in the morning. I was just about to doze at the drone of my own recorded message when I heard Grace's frantic voice crying, "Stanley. Oh, Stan, please wake up! Please, please wake up. This is Grace. Something terrible has happened. I need you. Please pick up! Please!"

I scrambled to the desk and grasped the receiver just as she was about to give up. On hearing my voice, she lapsed into sobs that did not abate until I was fully awake, which could have taken a long time, considering how soundly I had been sleeping.

"Grace," I cried, "what happened?"

"I made dinner!" she howled, as if she were confessing to a crime of passion. "I made *dinner*! I made the spaghetti. We had a lovely *dinner*!" she yelled, applying emphasis to words that seemed not to deserve it under any circumstances.

"Stanley," she shouted. "He *ate*! He ate, and he had a heart attack. He had a *heart* attack!"

Before I could stop myself, I heard the question leaking out of my mouth: "Grace, whose recipe? Was it your sauce or mine?"

"This is *no time* to do that to me!" she screamed, giving me credit that I did not deserve and precious time to recover from my own stupid question. "I *know* what you're doing. This is no time for tactics. This happened!"

"He ate your spaghetti and had a heart attack? Is he alive?"

"Yes! Yes, he's alive. He had the heart attack on top of me. He didn't have it at dinner! We were in bed! We were making love! The first time since Times Square was a meadow that I had a . . . oh, my God!"

Grace's illusions drifted back and forth between conventional reality and her private reality. I never successfully determined exactly what purpose they served, for instance, in periodically making her responsible for such global atrocities as the Vietnam War, but I did succeed in helping her wrest some control over their drifting, in giving her some power over the timing and frequency of the shifts from conventional reality to illusory reality. I suspect that in her private reality, she felt so responsible for events precisely because in her conventional reality, she felt so out of control regarding them. Her anxiety over the lack of control triggered the erection of an illusion, as a means of escaping or containing the anxiety.

Bob pulled through. After his triple-bypass surgery he and Grace moved in together. And after a few more frantic calls, spaced about two years apart, Grace stopped calling me.

I stopped inventing recipes, too.

POSTSCRIPT

I have a multilayered fondness for these two cases. To me, they represent important lessons learned, or at least observed, at a deliciously early stage in my career. I am charmed by memories of my relationship with these two women, and amused but not at all embarrassed by my youthful exuberance, energy, fervor, and optimism. I still laugh aloud when I ponder the hours I spent babbling gibberish to Florence, on the absurd notion that I might stumble across a syllabic combination that, pronounced correctly, would have a definition in her illusion's lexicon.

I also am amazed, now and then, at what I much later took to be Florence's fit of generosity toward me. Her taking the time and summoning the trust to utter, for the first time in years, one complete sentence for me, and then an elliptical answer, in English, amounted to a generous tip for all my seemingly wasted effort.

Partly because on budgetary constraints, no doubt, and partly because of Florence's relentlessly confounding behavior, traditional psychotherapy had abandoned Florence to daily physical caretaking and no more. Newly graduated therapists annually had sat opposite her blank gaze. They got nowhere and ultimately gave up. But she had seen and heard my ridiculously protracted effort, and she evidently judged it worthy of a heroic kindness. By speaking, at long last, she showed me that she knew and had known the language, that she could speak it if she felt so inclined, and therefore that she was very much in control of her world and the place she took in it. Then, by returning so abruptly to her previous demeanor, to her preferred universe, she showed me quite emphatically that she was being exactly what, where, and how she wanted to be, thank you very much.

Though I was not yet convinced of it at the time, both spaghetti cases illustrate my point about the value of therapists moving away from the position of being the outside observer and to a position more like that of the anthropologist, whose study requires that he imagine himself a participant in the daily life of a different society, the better to understand its rules and customs. Both cases also illustrate a point I later solidified as a working premise: that apparent problems are often solutions to less apparent problems.

Florence's revelation forced me to face the jarring truth that the reality I was trying to reintroduce her to—my reality—was evidently far less desirable than the reality she had created for herself. I was in no position to judge whether Florence would be happier or better off in my world than in hers, but inadvertently I had found out which world she preferred—a startling lesson for me, and unforgettable.

If Florence was content in her illusions, Grace was not. She was suffering, and I wanted to relieve her of at least some of her anguish. I did not know the origins or the specific functions of her illusions. It was very early in my career, and I did not yet understand that problems had functions. But with Grace, I was at least able to influence her control of the illusions, so that she suffered less anxiety for them. Under traditional circumstances, a psychiatrist might have given her a prescription or two and followed it up with years and years of psychoanalytic therapy designed to discover and then supplant whichever warps in her childhood development had led to her obsessions. But she already had been through a lot of that, and it had not made her life any better.

In respecting her universe to the point of absurdity, I created bigger fantasies than she, giving her a different perspective on her own fantasies and allowing her to minimize them to a more manageable extent. On a much smaller scale, we do exactly this with our children all the time, and it almost always calms them and makes their pain easier to bear. A child falls in the presence of his parent, skins his knee, spies the wound and screams as if he had been dismembered. Knowing that the same child has fallen the same way in a crowded playground without so drastic a reaction, the parent responds with a form of humor—essentially joining the child's exaggerated illusion and thus reducing the child's panic over the comparatively benign reality. "Let me see," says the parent. "Is the leg still attached? Yes. That's good. Is it broken? No, not broken. Good. If we fix this fast enough, you may live to play another day. What about the street? Is the street all right? Just a dent in the street. Good.

The policeman won't notice. Maybe a bandage would help, what do you think? Or should we see the doctor?''

Case closed. The child resumes play.

Do we know all the reasons for the child's behavior—why he dusts himself off and returns to his fellows in the playground but reacts differently when his parent is around? No. Do we even know why we instinctively join his illusion and then stretch it until it snaps back?

No, but we do it, and it works.

FATHER KNOWS
BEST

Chicago, 1987

"THIS IS A VERY TRADITIONAL MIDWESTERN FAMILY," SAID
Evelyn Ellis, a graduate therapist who had requested a consultation on a long-term case of hers. The family had just
arrived and was seated in a waiting room outside. Evelyn's
file was perched on her lap, but as she reviewed the case,
she didn't glance even once at the file. She knew the story
well.

"The father," she began, "Ted Townsend, is a free-lance
packaging designer and appears to be quite successful at it,
though it takes up a lot of his time because, well, he's almost like a free-lance artist or writer. He not only has to
create the product, he has to go out and obtain work, sell
his wares, his experience, his imagination, sell himself. So,
he has a lot of external pressure and stress, day to day. He
has a lot to worry about. But then, strangely, he also em-
braces a great deal of extra pressure at home, worrying
about the rest of his family, worrying about every detail of
their lives, in fact. I've been seeing this family for a long
time, and the father's constant worrying, his persistent anxiety, has the whole family on edge constantly, as if they all
were emotionally clenched all the time because of his internal tension about them and their welfare. Session after session, that's all they want to talk about. His anxiety pervades

the family and dominates it, and I am feeling very frustrated that I haven't been able to find a way to help alleviate their discomfort, because otherwise they present a nearly ideal American family.

"Let me add, by the way, that they love him; no question about it, his wife and two children, both adolescents, love him, and he loves them. But whenever he is not distracted by work, he's peppering every one of them, with questions about subjects like the children's performance in school, the way his wife drives the car, whether everyone uses seat belts, whether everybody is taking good care of their teeth, were they careful about the route they took home, did they listen to the weather reports—on and on. This year the oldest daughter is preparing to take the test for a driver's license, so he's been talking about that constantly. He reminds her every day about signaling before turning—and this at the dinner table. He must have told her four times that if she was in an accident while she was making a left turn, the accident was going to be her fault, according to the insurance companies, no matter what actually happened, because you're always at fault when you're breaking into traffic flow. Ask me how I know this so well. I've heard it repeated, so you can imagine how often the daughter hears it. He's got her so tense that she won't turn left if he's in the same town. He cautioned her to drive only a big car, so that she would be less likely to get seriously hurt in her first accident, like it's already a given. Here she is, staring down at French-cut green beans and a pork chop, and he practically has her programmed to have her first car accident and get it over with, when she hasn't even taken her driver's test yet.

"I have tried everything I can think of," Evelyn said. "I even consulted with a psychiatrist, who saw Ted once or twice, basically agreed with me, and gave him a prescription for an anti-anxiety drug—Xanax, I believe. But the Xanax has no appreciable effect, either, which amazes me, because I took a Xanax once, when both my parents had been in an auto accident, and it's a very powerful item. But on this man? Zero. It has no effect. Nothing seems to ease his anxiety."

Thus warned that both the therapist and the entire family had become completely focused on the father's worrying as the primary problem for everyone, I chose my course. I determined to first diffuse that view if I could, because it did not seem to be leading anywhere, and then to look for another opportunity. I asked Evelyn if she would mind my suggesting that she observe my initial encounter with the family from outside the room, through the one-way mirror, so that she could distance herself from the situation. Evelyn had no objection, but when I approached the family, introduced myself, and offered exactly that as my first suggestion, Ted Townsend immediately spoke up, seemingly as the representative of the entire family, and said, "We would be very anxious about that. I would like Evelyn to sit in with us, even if she were acting only as an observer this time."

I had not addressed the question to him. I had asked everyone, making sure I made eye contact with the mother, Joan, a haphazardly dressed woman with short dark hair; the son, Wayne, a fifteen-year-old blond, athletic-looking young man; the daughter, Sarah, seventeen, also blond and quite lovely in a plain, wholesome way; and Ted, a balding, baby-faced man, neatly dressed, overweight, his bifocals perched precariously but somehow fastidiously on the end of his tiny nose.

It seemed that everyone in the family was in accord with Ted's anxiety about Evelyn's participation, though only he had articulated it. So if the whole family was equally anxious, then Ted might be the person who articulated the entire family's anxiety, not just his own. No one had disagreed with him. So my first suspicion was that the anxiety that everyone had identified as Ted's problem might be an expression of the family's problem.

Respecting that anxiety, which I took to be the whole family's, I agreed that Evelyn could stay in the room, but then said, "Tell me, why does everyone here think that Evelyn decided to invite me in to meet you?" Immediately Ted answered, "She wants to get some fresh input, no doubt."

"She's probably frustrated," said Joan, her voice taut. "After all, she's tried everything."

"Evelyn's gotten very attached to us," Ted offered, as if protecting her. "It's difficult for her to deal with us when we've become such good friends."

"She's like a grandmother, then," I said, thinking about their protectiveness toward their therapist and about how mutually protective this family felt overall, even to the point of embracing their therapist.

Finally I asked the family the standard opening question: "So, what do you think the current problem is, anyway?"

Ted shot a quick glance at Joan and said, not as a question but as a declaration, "You want me to go first."

I took the remark to be a protective maneuver. I was the outsider; he was going to absorb whatever might be the impact of the first encounter with me. He then continued, fully embracing the family's problem as his own.

"I'm having a tough time with the kids," he said. "They're growing older, and I can't always protect them. They're in a hurry to be independent, and they rebel, like all kids do, I'm sure. They don't want to hear me. But they have to. They're kids still, and they can only take so much."

"What is your reaction when they rebel?" I asked. "When they don't want to hear you?"

"Well," he mused, with a slight touch of self-consciousness, "I guess I feel like I've failed as a father."

"In what way?"

"Well, I guess I'm a fairly old-fashioned guy family-wise. It may seem funny to some people in this modern world, but when I think of family, my mind goes back to the best of the family TV shows, like *Ozzie and Harriet* and *Leave It to Beaver*, when people always talked out their problems and then agreed to behave in a certain, wholesome way toward each other, when there were no arguments, no fights, no sarcasm. I love that idea of family life, or that ideal, but we just don't have that. Maybe you can't have it. Maybe nobody can, but we certainly don't.''

Aware now of his increasingly obvious role as the guardian of the family, I asked Ted if he would mind my asking his children the same question as I had asked him: what did they think the problem was in the family? He gave me his permission. Sarah meanwhile seemed defiantly bored as she twirled a lock of her hair and stared off into the distance, so I addressed Wayne first.

Wayne looked at his father and ventured, ''He worries all the time about everything I do. Whatever it is, wherever it is, whenever it is. It's like being watched. It really gets on my nerves.''

''Maybe that's his way of protecting you,'' I said. ''He seems to me to be extremely protective.''

Suddenly Sarah interrupted, ''Whenever I'm watching television,'' she said, ''and something bad happens to somebody—like a person in a story gets hurt, or mugged, or crashes a car—my father says to me, 'That could happen to you, you know.' Or 'That's probably what's going to happen to you.' I mean, like, give me a break, please.''

I said I understood her consternation. ''But wouldn't you agree,'' I added, ''that the world could be a dangerous place sometimes, and that you might need the kind of protection your father is offering, or is hoping to be able to offer? Don't you think you might need his protection, even want it?''

''I suppose,'' she said. ''Yes, in fact. Yes. I just don't want to be smothered in it.''

Then I asked a question that had been puzzling me since the beginning of the exchange. ''What about Mom, Sarah? Does she worry, too?''

''No,'' she said flatly.

''Not at all? Never? Your dad takes all the responsibility for worrying.''

''Well, I don't give her much to worry about. I don't do things to worry her.''

"But every parent worries a little," I prodded.

Sarah was becoming very uncomfortable. I think the rest of the family was, too. They seemed surprised and chagrined that we suddenly were discussing Joan, as if she were off-limits.

"Oh, my mom just sort of floats around all day," Sarah said as she squirmed slightly in her chair. "She'll start to clean the house, but then she'll get into a crossword puzzle."

She paused, as if she had gone too far. Then she decided to keep going.

"So, the house is a mess, if you really want to know," she said. "It's a sty. My mother just isn't very organized. She's funny. She'll go an hour out of her way to take advantage of double coupons for groceries, using up in gasoline twice the amount she saved, and using up three times the amount of time. That's where her time goes, out the window. She's pretty disorganized."

"I'm getting the impression that your mother doesn't worry about anything, while your father worries about everything," I said. "You have two very interesting parents: one who worries all the time, and one who doesn't worry at all."

I turned to Ted and asked, "How is it that you let her off the hook so easily? Your wife, I mean. It's really very noble of you to do all the worrying. You take on this burden and allow your wife to be free from it. But I can't help but wonder why it is so important to you that she is free from worry. Let me ask you a question. If Joan were to worry at all, what would you think she would worry about?"

"Her mother," Ted said after a long pause. "Her mother lives in New Jersey. She's old. She's alone. Joan's father died five years ago. Joan gets very anxious about her mother. I see the long-distance calls on the phone bill. She calls New Jersey often."

"So she's close to her mother."

"Yes. If anything were to happen to her mother, Joan would no doubt hit the panic button."

"So, Ted," I said, now conscious of this man's self-sacrificial habit of distracting his disorganized, anxious wife from spiraling through her own worries. "I take it you worry a great deal about your wife?"

He looked at me as if surprised, and then shrugged as if on second thought he merely had heard me state the obvious.

"Yes, I do," he said. "I worry about her all the time. Everybody else thinks I spend all my spare time worrying about the kids, and, all right, I worry about the kids on weekends," he added, chuckling. "But Joan, I worry about her all week long. I do. Honestly. Every day. You're absolutely right."

Joan watched him intently, wide-eyed, like a squirrel pausing between bursts of movement.

"And she gives you plenty to worry about," I added.

Everyone laughed, Joan with a stiffened sort of relief.

"If something happened to her mother, Ted, do you think that Joan really would fall apart?"

Ted paused again.

"If her mother were to pass on? Is that what you mean? Oh, sure. For certain. I worry about that, her falling apart. She holds a lot in, my Joan, and it's not easy to pick up the hints. But I've known her a long, long time, and I believe it's entirely possible that if something happened with her mother, Joan could drop right off the edge."

Joan twitched and grimaced involuntarily. The kids now were watching her intently.

"Has she ever done it?" I asked. "Has she ever lost it, dropped off the edge?"

"Well, it's not that she's run off screaming into the night, but, well . . . this is hard—I hope this doesn't hurt you, my saying this—but there are signs sometimes. Joan will all of a sudden announce at ten-thirty at night that she's going shopping, for instance. Well, all right, other people go shopping at night, but usually they plan it, or they're people who have daytime jobs. It isn't some impulsive thing. They don't just go off to the all-night supermarket because it's ten-thirty. I mean, like, Joan has spent hours in the middle of the night cleaning the attic! I swear, I'm not making this up—she takes stuff out of the attic and brings it down to the garage to be ready for the weekly rubbish pickup—at three o'clock in the morning. I mean, when it happens, I don't have a good sense of where she is. And, yeah, it frightens me a little, and I worry about that. I do worry about her. She's my wife.''

I nodded. I was very moved, frankly, and impressed. I said I needed a few moments to organize my thoughts, but that I did have ideas I wanted to convey to them before they left. I said I would like to exchange some of these ideas with Evelyn, because I knew of their concern for her, and I said that if they could take a recess and give me ten or twenty minutes, I would like to speak again to them briefly.

I took my break. I thought about the case, exchanged some ideas with Evelyn, and returned to the room to tell them what was on my mind.

I addressed myself to Ted.

''I'm very impressed with you,'' I said. ''You have been doing such a thorough job of taking on the full-time burden as the worrier for your family that I can't tell you what deep respect I have for who you are and what you've done. I think you've been doing a job that this family has needed done rather desperately, and I think that you've taken it on despite the difficult role it has placed you in and its consequences. It evidently has made you the perceived source of the very problems you have protected everyone else from. You have done all the worrying for your entire family, with the ironic consequence that the family sees your worrying as the problem it is most worried about. It is remarkable what you have accomplished.

''Thank you,'' he said. ''I appreciate your saying that.''

''Not only that,'' I said, ''I particularly admire how you

managed to recognize that your wife has needed you in a very profound way, and how faithful you have been in your concern for her and her peace of mind.''

''Thank you again,'' he said, with heartfelt sincerity.

I continued, ''You have given Joan license to be carefree, free-spirited, while you've functioned as the mother hen, worrying about the children as if you were both parents, not just one. Yet I know that you have been worried, too, about what would happen to her if you were not protecting her, about whether without you, she might not go off the deep end, or panic, or become dangerously disorganized. By providing the right amount of distraction for her and then taking the brunt of her criticism, you have created the illusion that you are the source of the family's discomfort. You are not. You've provided a smokescreen.

''I think it might be important for you and everybody else in the family if you were to find out just what would happen if you were not there to distract your wife from her worries. I believe that your worrying has been very valuable to her, and I don't think you should give it up entirely. It occurs to me, as I am telling you this, that it makes perfect sense now why you would not have responded to your medication. Your body will not allow you to abdicate this role that you have embraced. It would be too dangerous. So, I don't think you should give up worrying entirely—I think your worrying probably is necessary—until we know what direction your wife's behavior will take if you are not doing all the worrying. So, you should worry some, but I would like to recommend that you contain your worrying to, say, one hour a day.''

Ted laughed. Then the kids laughed.

''I'm serious. When do you worry the most?''

''When I come home from work.''

''Okay, I'd like you to worry every day, as you have been, but instead of at random, do it for one hour, and in the presence of your wife, so that she can be reassured. You will continue therefore to have this job at least part-time, and while you're protecting your wife, you'll also have plenty of other time to go about your life, maybe even seek some pleasure. In this way you'll be able to continue to remain faithful and protective but without worrying all the time. You've been so extremely helpful and protective, but with the consequence that you haven't had much fun."

"That's true," Ted nearly whispered.

"Perhaps we also will be able to find out what Joan is so afraid of, and what will happen to her."

"I'm out of practice at not worrying," said Ted.

I grinned. "I have confidence in you," I said. "Anyway, it's like riding a bike. Once you learn how not to worry, you never forget the rudiments."

He smiled. It was a broad and captivating smile of recognition, acceptance, enrichment, and gratitude. It filled me up.

While my solution seemed like a quick fix for what was perceived to be the problem between Ted and his children, I knew that his recognizing the usefulness of his anguish was going to result in a profound change in his perception of himself, and in the other family members' perception of both him and themselves individually. No one could expect that he would stop worrying immediately, even according to a schedule he would prescribe for himself, but in time, I thought, he might stop. And then his wife would have to assume the responsibility for her own worrying.

Once again I had learned that the problem in a family was not a problem but an attempt at solving a problem. Changing the way the family attempted to cope with Joan's anxiety and her disorganized approach was bound to have consequences. I knew that and suggested as much. If reorganizing Ted's worrying meant he and the children were going to be liberated to a certain degree from its weight and constancy, someone would wind up with the slack, and it would have to be Joan. Because of the entire family's mutual protectiveness, the process no doubt would take time, but it would happen.

Seven months later, I received a telephone call from Joan, who was visiting her mother in New Jersey. She said her whole life was topsy-turvy, and she wanted to see me. She said that Ted pretty much had stopped worrying, and now she was worrying, and she didn't think she could handle the burden.

I said I thought it would be unwise for me to see her without seeing the rest of the family at the same time. "I know how your family works," I told her. "It would be too much of a betrayal to see you without them present." I promised I would schedule an appointment for the entire family the next time I was in Chicago. I gave her a date for my next visit and the telephone number of the place I expected to be staying.

They never called. I don't know exactly what happened, though the therapist who first consulted me did tell me that the family had managed months before to construct an adaptation to accommodate Joan's anxiety. She had not seen them, either, since around the time of Joan's call to me. I am confident that if Joan reached a point where she absolutely could not bear her burdens, her family would have found a way to spare her. Since she did not call again, she and her family more than likely conspired either consciously or otherwise to design a fine alteration in the pattern, which ultimately protected her. And of course, Evelyn, their therapist-"grandmother," would always be on hand.

POSTSCRIPT

This morality play of a case is an elegant example of how a family—parents and children together—colluded to create an illusion that protected one parent from an overdose of anxiety by targeting the other and unconsciously conspiring parent to exaggerate his place in the family.

The configuration is very common in families; sometimes

a spouse sacrifices himself, sometimes a child or a grandparent. While it is usually an act of devotion on the part of the member who deflects the negative attention by absorbing it himself, if the sacrifice extends over time, it can become a self-sacrifice that wears away at a person's hopes and dreams.

The fiction that the family creates often serves to stabilize the family in response to unidentified threats to that stability. The "Achieving Failure" section of this book contains other examples. This case happens to be a fairly extreme example, wherein the father evidently showed his willingness to take on the pivotal negative role, and all of the children joined wholeheartedly in the conspiracy, protecting the troubled, anxious mother from the residual effects of her anxiety over her own mother.

I don't think there was anything particularly dramatic about my intervention in this case, but the pattern is so common and yet so commonly overlooked, that the family almost always is surprised at my approach and my discoveries. When I see such a rigid and universally accepted description of a symptomatic member of a family, with almost no deviation on anyone's part, I know both theoretically and intuitively that the family is telling me a kind of useful fiction. If everyone agrees with the story, it's almost certainly a meaningful conspiracy that masks another story. If they all agree that they have identified the problem, the problem they have identified probably is hiding a greater problem. So, I can immediately begin a search for who and what their conspiratorial story is protecting, and when I detect it, I try to unbalance the artificial equilibrium they have created with their mythology. Once the family members are jarred loose from their agreed-upon myth, they have the opportunity to be as creative in forming new interactions as they were in forming their presenting problem.

SIN'S SYNDROME

Long Island, New York, Spring 1979

CHERYL BAKER ENTERED THE ROOM CRADLING A NEWBORN wrapped in pink. She directed three other children to the seats nearest the one she had claimed with her pocketbook and baby bag. The older children were scrubbed and polished, fastidiously dressed, and as well behaved as any I had seen. They sat upright, folded their hands in their laps, and smiled hesitantly at me and Bernard Waller, a young family practice resident whose training I was supervising at a family studies center. Other trainees were observing from behind a two-way mirror, but I had asked Bernard to accompany me because of a medical notation on the intake memorandum.

The oldest of Cheryl Baker's children, a boy who was about ten, noticed his mother struggling with her equipment and jumped to remove the bag and pocketbook from the chair, a simple, unaffected gesture that spoke paragraphs about at least this child's relationship with his mother, who obviously had inspired this generosity.

"Is your husband joining us?" I asked. "Should we wait, or are we all here?"

"My husband couldn't get off work today," she said with a weak but gentle smile that I took to mean that the husband did not want to come, or maybe didn't know she had made an appointment. I would have preferred otherwise, but he wasn't there, and I couldn't do much about it.

"Well, why don't we begin, then?" I said. "I have a cryptic note here that suggests that you're having problems with the baby. Why don't you tell me what brought you here?"

She looked down at the baby, then at the floor. The room fell silent, as the older children watched their mother with a worried intensity. Talking more or less to the floor, Cheryl said quietly and plaintively, "I need to know how to take care of her. The baby."

My first reaction was surprise. After all, she evidently had raised three older children from infancy.

"The baby is more difficult than your other children were at that stage," I declared.

She nodded affirmatively.

"Well, what is the greatest difficulty with this baby? Let's start there."

"She has Down's Syndrome," Cheryl said ever so slowly.

The four-word utterance had significant impact. Right away I could imagine the dramatic change this family would go through, the disruption of life as they had lived it. My mind raced ahead to sacrifices that ranged in intensity from unfair inconvenience to genuine suffering. I hadn't taken a good look at the infant, but now I was straining to see her face.

"Oh," I said. "When did you learn this?"

Cheryl answered softly, staring down at the bundle in her lap. "Well," she said, "I read an article about it a couple of weeks ago."

My brow raised. She saw my expression and continued.

"I read an article in the *Reader's Digest*," she said. "It was about birth defects in babies, like Down's Syndrome babies. It said that babies who have Down's Syndrome have very wide spaces between their toes. And so I looked at her toes, and she has these very wide spaces between her toes."

She snapped the sentence shut, raised her chin, and

looked directly into my eyes. The other children looked up at me. Bernard looked at me.

The *Reader's Digest*, I thought. Friend and adviser to seventeen million Americans. Case cited, case closed. I tried not to reveal my surprise. I guess I expected the name of a doctor, followed by a symptomatic synopsis of his diagnosis. I looked over at Bernard. For a slightly wrong reason I was accompanied by the perfect co-therapist. I felt very lucky.

"Cheryl," I said gently, "my colleague, Bernard, here, is a physician. Do you mind if he examines your baby? What is the baby's name?"

"Catherine," she said, rising, unwrapping the baby, and presenting her to Bernard. "Cathy," she added, speaking directly to him.

Bernard took Catherine, his left hand cradling her back and neck, his right hand holding her bottom. He hefted her slightly, watching her limbs. Later he explained to me that he was looking immediately for weak muscle tone, floppy arms, legs, and head. He asked Cheryl if her daughter looked at her when she approached. Cheryl said yes. Meanwhile, the infant appeared to be focusing on Bernard already. Bernard asked if Cathy smiled yet. "Now and then, anyway?" he said.

"Oh, yes," she said. "All the time."

"How does she feed?" Bernard asked, while touching the back of his pinky to Cathy's lips, which promptly pursed and closed around Bernard's finger. "Is she a slow feeder, compared to what you remember of your older children at this stage?"

"No, she drains her formula bottles real good."

He asked about bowel movements. Cheryl said that Cathy's bowel movements were fine. The kids giggled.

Bernard looked intently at Cathy's face. He felt around the back of her head, all the while cooing and watching her eyes follow his.

He touched and probed, unsnapped and snapped Cathy's

stretchie, and finally glanced over at me with an ever so slight shrug and a raised brow. The physical examination was as complete as possible, and nothing was wrong with this baby. I said, "Thank you, Bernard."

I looked at Cheryl, truly puzzled. What ever would make so obviously capable a mother create a private diagnosis of Down's Syndrome in her beautiful and healthy newborn? And how could I pry this illusion's function from her thoughts, let alone without scaring the children?

Looking at the oldest child, as if to suggest that he and I were co-conspiring to free his mother from her problem, I tilted my head slightly, leaned back, and rose from my chair. I recalled a similar case involving Carl Whittaker, a pioneer family therapist at the University of Wisconsin's Department of Medicine, in which he used a ruler to disrupt an illusion. This intervention was radical and I would duplicate it in an attempt to dislodge an absurd illusion with an equally absurd examination. All eyes followed as I stepped to the two-way mirror and rapped my knuckles against it with as much pompous authority as I could muster.

"Bring me a ruler!" I commanded. "Look in my top desk drawer." I glanced back at the boy and nodded, even half winked, as if to suggest, "*We* will get to the bottom of this!" He stared bug-eyed at me, but the other two stared in admiration at him.

An observing therapist entered the room and gave me a wooden ruler.

"Everyone please take off your shoes and socks," I said. "You, too, Bernard." I smacked the ruler against my hand, looked at the boy again, looking thoughtfully at my feet, then began to deliberately remove my own shoes.

The kids reacted eagerly. I whispered to them, "My mother is going to be so happy that I'm not wearing socks with holes in the toes." They smiled, while their mother struggled to bend over past the baby to remove her shoes.

Trailing a clipboard and a pen in my left hand and the ruler in my right, I got down on my hands and knees. I started with Bernard, measuring the toes of his left foot first, then his right, and the spaces between each toe. Writing down the results as if I were taking inventory of state secrets, I repeated the measurements with each child, then with Cheryl, then with little Cathy, then myself, asking the boy to hold the clipboard and transcribe my calculations. I retrieved my clipboard, returned to my chair, took a calculator out of my pocket, and began punching in numbers. Finally I looked up at the children, took a deep breath, and sighed. Glancing first over at Bernard, then back at the kids, I said, "It appears from these measurements that my colleague, Bernard, has Down's Syndrome."

The older boy let escape a short burst of laughter, freeing his sisters to giggle along, freeing me to laugh just behind them, freeing Cheryl and Bernard, in that order, to fairly collapse in an unburdening laughter that lasted nearly twenty seconds.

Cheryl seemed a little nervous. In what must have been a profound moment of recognition she said, "You know what I think? I think I imagined a problem with the baby. I might have made it up in my head because she was so different from the other three. This is something probably only I knew about, or even know about: that Cathy's features were so different—I mean, eyes, hair—you could look at her and say, you know, she's a beautiful baby, but where did she come from? Maybe you would see a little of me in there, but you couldn't find a trace of Tom, her father, you know?"

Now it made sense. This child *was* different, a secret Cheryl believed could devastate her life. Her perfect illusion covered her worst fears.

Now that she seemed ready, even eager, to confront her fears, I suddenly had to protect the children, who may not have been so ready. I interrupted, saying, "Excuse me, but these young people have been awfully patient with us." Looking at the oldest again, my comrade, I asked, "Would you children prefer to relax in the waiting room while your mom talks with Bernard and me a little while longer? We have another room in here with a TV, and I think nobody's using it now. Would you want to go there for a few minutes?''

The kids all nodded.

With the children gone, Cheryl continued.

''You probably can guess that there was a reason for that, which there was. It almost feels like I've been hiding it for so long that I must have hidden it from myself, as impossible as that seems. So what I must have done was . . . I mean, the fourth child was so different, and obviously—*now* obviously, anyway—that there had been a problem.

''So I made the baby have a problem instead of having the problem be the problem. And now I don't know what to do.''

She then told a fairly conventional story about a couple who had gradually drifted toward all the distractions of a marriage and away from all its attractions, like attentiveness, tenderness, and, ultimately, passion. While she was agonizing over whether Tom's romantic interests had been piqued elsewhere, another man began to pay particular attention to her. The result was Catherine, and with the news of her conception, the end of the affair.

''So your guilt led you to believe strongly that something must be wrong with the baby,'' I said. ''Do you know that this ability to organize an illusion as a defense against reality is not so unusual? It isn't. And it's very powerful.''

''I haven't faced anything very well, have I?'' she said. ''Not anything.''

''I don't know about that,'' Bernard said. ''I think you're doing quite well at the moment, don't you?''

''Bernard is right,'' I said. ''You just walked yourself out of a very powerful illusion. You just did that yourself. And you brought yourself here to do it.''

She smiled weakly, sighed, and declared, ''I did, didn't I? That's a nice thought. I need to believe that. I think when I was watching you examine the baby and ask me all those questions, I knew something was ending, or lifting. What do I do now, though? I don't know what to do."

"Do you think you might ask your husband to come back with you for another appointment?" I asked, adding, "I think it might be a good idea myself."

She sighed again, half determined, half resigned.

"Yes," she said after a pause. "I'll talk to him. I will. But what should I tell him?"

I shrugged. "Tell him," I said, "that you've made an appointment."

I felt she had taken a big enough step for the moment in freeing herself from the illusions that had served to free her from a difficult truth. We would deal with that in other sessions, with her husband present. The immediate problem, now solved through a little gentle humor and absurdity, was the illusion she had created to handle her intense anxiety about the consequences of her actions, even to thwart her own recognition of her actions.

I saw her illusion as a kind of a metaphor for the illegitimacy of her child. Somehow it balanced the past and the future, made everything sum up correctly in her mind, and acted as a kind of guardian, protecting her from her own secret. Continuing to operate under the protection of the illusion would have created a greater and more absurd disaster in the future. So, an absurd intervention was used to budge the absurd illusion.

POSTSCRIPT

Cheryl Baker's illusion provided one of those rare opportunities to apply a procedure learned in the classroom to a remarkably similar situation of my own, and then to enjoy the wonderful experience of watching it work in a truly meaningful way. The technique was a variation on a theme I had been exploring since my days of graduate study—since the time, in fact, of the ''Spaghetti Stories''—the idea of joining someone's universe, of extending illusions to an absurd length in an effort to yank their author back to a more manageable reality.

Cheryl's was an extreme illusion, but she knew she had a problem—a new child and its accompanying secret to contend with. More commonly people create illusions by denying the existence of a problem or by erasing the clear indications of trouble, as in the alcoholic or drug-addicted family, where the alcoholic says there is no problem and the enabler is always creating or nurturing the illusion that the problems do not exist. But whether the problem is an identifiable illusion or the illusion is the denial of an identifiable problem, I seek to understand how the illusion functions in the context of the family relationship, and what the consequences of dislodging the illusion would be.

Cheryl Baker believed her baby had Down's Syndrome when the baby did not. I had to find out what the meaning of the illusion was, to begin to speculate on the consequences of her surrendering the illusion. The technique I chose was as metaphorically theatrical as the illusion itself. I could not use language and logic because they were not the tools with which she had created the illusion. So, an intervention that might seem to be have been a moment of inspiration was actually based on a pretty clear map, one that I had learned about and developed over many years of practice and recalled, in a specific way, from another clinician's case.

Once we established, through the context of lightness and humor, that the baby's Down's Syndrome was an illusion, that the baby was illegitimate, and that Cheryl was terrified of the consequences of revealing her secret, we could begin to deal with all of it from a different perspective.

THE
HETEROPHOBIC
MAN

New York, 1990

OTHER PEOPLE HAD ENTERED MY OFFICES AND SUGGESTED TO me that they were failing in life—at their jobs, at their relationships, at whatever were their expectations for themselves—but their punctuating body language and their general deportment, had always reflected varying levels of frustration, anger, despondency, even embarrassment. Roger Birney, by contrast, seemed so thoroughly ashamed that his demeanor unsettled me. I merely had asked him what I might have asked anyone else on the initial encounter. I was looking for what I called the "presenting problem," asking the troubled to identify the trouble. He had bowed his head in response, turning slightly away to his right. He breathed a short, empty sigh and seemed to focus on some spot miles beneath the floor. My imagination may have been contributing, but the corners of his mouth seemed to have fallen to match his sunken shoulders. His posture fell beyond sadness or even depression and descended into humiliation and shame.

He began speaking almost inaudibly, as if a dentist's injection had numbed his lips and vocal cords. He paused uncomfortably between phrases. "I think the problem . . . is . . . that I'm just not any good," he said, "not for myself, not for anybody else. I'm just not any good." He looked up at me. His dark eyes were sad and deep. The act of raising his head seemed to have taken all the strength he could muster, though he lowered it just as slowly.

Information leaked out slowly, too, but he did begin to tell me about himself—a man incapable of making commitments, he judged; a thirty-eight-year-old man who had spent most of his adult life failing at relationships with women; a man currently involved with a woman from whom he felt increasingly estranged, and who in fact had encouraged him to make the appointment with me.

He had been trained as a paralegal. He had earned an associate's degree by painting and wallpapering in the daytime and attending school at night. He had managed to land a decent job in his chosen field, although he said he had ruined that, too, by becoming romantically involved with the seventeen-year-old daughter of one of the law firm's wealthiest and most respected clients. He was fired for it. In another law firm, he said, his rebelliousness forced him to resign. I tried not to look startled by the notion of this so humiliated-looking man being rebellious. He said he would not conform to the law firm's rules and its structure. He characterized his behavior there as stubborn and defiant. It seemed so incongruous at the moment. Later I would find it possible to imagine him as passively defiant, like the child who steadfastly refuses to join the rest of his class in a song. But Roger admitted, too, that he had been manifestly unpopular among the clerks, secretaries, paralegals, and attorneys in both of the first two law firms and that his continuing feeling of unpopularity—real or imagined—had led him to quit a third job in the field.

His relationships with women were no more successful than in law firms. He said that he had walked away from any number of girlfriends, even, on two occasions, fiancées. His departure from the relationships always was abrupt, struck his prospective partners as an absolute surprise, and made him feel even more ashamed. He had pretty much convinced himself that he was utterly selfish and unworthy, and that his current girlfriend's estimation of him possibly was just, and probably not severe enough.

In keeping with his own view of himself—or so I guessed, anyway—he now was working full-time as a limousine driver rather than as a paralegal. He felt it no use to seek a fourth job in a law office; the prospective employer would only ask the former firms about his worth, and he had proven unworthy. So he planted himself one step above a cabbie, he said, and settled. I could not accept his occupational condemnation, but I kept quiet about it. In prior marital counseling I had encountered a truck driver, a cabdriver, and a sanitation worker who were fiercely proud of their roles and their contributions. The sanitation man in particular spoke with pride about his strength, speed, and reliability. He clearly felt a fraternal pride in his association with an identifiable department of the city workforce. The cabdriver frequently had to be stopped from regaling me and his estranged wife with wonderfully bizarre stories of his more celebrated fares.

Roger's shame could not be a function of his station, so I had to learn more about the origin of his easy condemnation of himself in this role. I asked him what line of work his father was trained in, and he said that his father was a sanitation worker, which he quickly reduced linguistically to "garbageman." He said his mother had to work part-time cleaning other apartments in order for the family to survive, and that she worked at all was a source of great shame for his father. His father's siblings had fared much better in life, and the comparison always wore heavily on Roger's father. One owned a replacement window business, another was a pharmacist. Not reminding Roger's father of his apparent, comparative failures was a theme within the Birney household. His mother's frequent refrain, he recalled, was: "Let's not give Daddy any more to worry about. He has enough already."

The initial session thus was ending in some mystery. It would deepen. I did not yet know of Roger's sexual torment, or of the part of his life that society would have considered sordid and aberrant, or of the exquisitely twisted anguish he suffered for what I eventually would judge to be a perfectly inverted, and therefore perfectly wrong, prior psychiatric diagnosis. Another mental health professional had led Roger to accept a self-evaluation founded on a destructively faulty premise, one that already had been officially adopted and later, finally, officially discarded by the psychiatric establishment. Unfortunately, many practitioners still held it dangerously dear, including the one Roger had consulted and believed for seven painful years of his adult life.

Ignorant of all of this, I concluded the session by trying to turn inside out what he perceived as his problem, to alter his viewpoint and perhaps allow him to begin revising his bleak self-perception. As gently as I could, I suggested the possibility that his shame reflected a certain loyalty to his father's shame. I said that the most obvious pattern I had seen so far was a steadfast refusal to rise above the level of his father's success. "In fact," I said, "I wonder if, as in a tradition of downwardly mobile men, you haven't succeeded in burdening yourself with even more shame than your father feels. It seems to me that what you consider your selfish behavior may actually be motivated by self-denial. You may be unwilling to own up to what you actually want, and instead deny all your own desires in the service of protecting your father, in not adding to his burden, just as your mother pleaded. That way you manage to prevent yourself from becoming yet another family member who torments him by surpassing him. That seems very self-sacrificial, doesn't it?"

I tried to say it all in a much more tentative way than I normally would, because he seemed so tentative a man to begin with. When I finished, I actually held my breath, almost frightened by his frailty.

He raised his eyes first, then lowered them, then raised his head. He looked straight at me, inhaled, and sighed, but he kept his head up and his eyes fixed on mine. He expelled a sort of quick, involuntary snort that terminated in the suggestion of a grin, a slight smile of new recognition, as if my suggestions not only were recognizable but potentially acceptable and even restorative. In retrospect, it was a powerful moment.

He confirmed my more optimistic suspicions at the beginning of the second session, saying outright that he was quite moved by the idea that what he had thought was selfish behavior might actually be self-denial. He had been thinking about it all week while driving the limo. He couldn't shake the thought. He looked a little stronger, though still defeated.

"It wouldn't explain everything, I suppose," he said, gazing at the floor again. "Some things . . . I don't know. Sometimes people just do things, behave in ways that they probably ought not to behave . . . and there's no . . . well, there must be explanations, aren't there? You would know about that."

Roger shuffled his feet and squirmed in his chair. He struggled pathetically to continue the thought—whatever it was—and seemed unable to. He spoke some more about self-denial. "I never thought of myself that way," he said. "It's such a different way of looking at it. I've talked to my girlfriend about it, and she said, 'Yeah, yeah, it makes sense. Even down to denying the pleasure of our relationship, denying sex, and all of that.'"

"Denying sex?" I asked. "In what way?"

"Oh, well, I'm not particularly turned on by her right now. I don't know why. Maybe I'm denying myself that kind of pleasure for the reasons you suggested."

"Well, if you're not turned on by her right now, what does turn you on, if anything?"

Roger's shuffling and squirming resumed in earnest. He cleared his throat, rubbed his chin, ran his fingers through his hair, and examined all the ceiling molding his eyes could reach without turning his head a full three hundred and sixty degrees. I decided to allow the silence and awkwardness to continue and so contributed nothing in the way of coaching or encouragement. Finally he began by telling me that he thought he had been denying his heterosexuality, punishing himself somehow by denying his girlfriend's advances or even his own natural longings. He then revealed that he had been punctuating that self-denial by secretly indulging in behavior that he carefully said could only be termed homosexual, mainly—and now he quickened the pace of his revelations—by offering oral sex to truck drivers at rest stops along the interstate, or strangers in public men's rooms, or cruising gay men in back alleys and parks. It only had made him more ashamed of himself, he said, though he seemed slightly more animated when he was enumerating the encounters, almost as if he wanted to describe them in more detail.

"Is that just recent, your engaging in that sort of activity?" I asked.

Answering that question absorbed a great deal of time, but he eventually revealed that he had been in therapy in the past, for seven years, ending two years before, he said, and that the homosexual interludes had been an integral part of his shameful life for many years and the primary subject of his therapy. I did not respond, but waited through his discomfort again. He repeated that his sexual behavior was the focus of seven years of prior therapy, almost as if he were begging me to address it. "I understood all of what my therapist told me," he said. "I understood the theory, the origin of the sickness. I understood it, but I didn't change anything. I guess it just didn't take, therapy-wise."

I remained silent.

After a minute or so, he said, "My therapist thought I was afraid of women. That was about seven years ago. Maybe I was just denying myself that pleasure."

The scenario was getting complicated. I asked him about his therapy. He said his therapist believed that his homosexual activities, his homosexual attractions, were symptomatic of whatever emotional or psychological disease afflicted him. In his psychiatric construct, the therapist implied that Roger's father's distant and sometimes hostile behavior toward him was a reaction to Roger's attachment to his mother, which his father envied. So, Roger's behavior reflected the lack of resolution of the classic oedipal dilemma. In the face of his father's rejection, said the therapist, Roger rejected his mother, along with his erotic attraction to her. This of course was systematically repressed, so that all that remained conscious were his rejection of women and his desire to please men. In that way his homosexuality was framed as a developmental disability. He had grown into what the therapist called a heterophobic man.

Already entrenched in a tradition of shame, Roger had found his therapist's definition very suitable. It enabled him then to carry out his ''illegitimate,'' or ''sick'' sexual behavior because he had no control over those urges, because they were part of a progressive disease. He thus gained from his so-called disease an alternating combination of arousal and shame, arousal and shame, a particularly powerful combination for him specifically because of his family background.

At the end of the second session, I was struggling with my own intellectual and emotional reactions to the damage I had seen done, to Roger Birney and to many others, by psychotherapists' loyalty to a psychiatric construct that had long since sunk out of sight. Years ago, the notion of heterophobia became the accepted psychiatric reasoning that explained homosexuality and thus led the American Psychiatric Association officially to designate homosexuality a mental illness, one which could be cured through proper treatment. Homosexuality thus had a diagnostic label and a category number, and its treatment could be reimbursed through third-party payment. The entire construct was reversed after many years, when in 1973 the association rescinded the designation and accepted instead the possibility that homosexuality was biologically and/or genetically based. Gay men and lesbians were who and what they were, to the credit or blame of no one. Despite the lifting of the official diagnosis, however, many psychoanalysts still held on to the theory—belief, really—that sexual preference was a preference, not a fact.

At the beginning of our third session, I asked Roger for a detailed accounting of his homosexual desires, fantasies, and experiences from as far back as he could remember. Initially he told me of incidents from his adolescence, masturbation sessions with other boys, some of which involved experimental touching and kissing under the guise of practicing for later encounters with girls. As he thought more about it, however, he remembered more—that from the age of five or six, he had favored the presence of men and was comforted by their proximity. He even recalled being identified by other adults as well as children as having characteristics and preferences more like a girl's than a boy's, though in adulthood he had not a trace of effeminacy. He remembered being physically drawn to the sights, sounds, and scents of men. He told me one vignette that had remained one of the fondest of his early childhood memories, wherein his father had taken him to a public pool and into the men's locker room. As he grew older, he recalled the incident with increasing fondness and eventually with a sense of eroticism. Next, he revealed that his fantasies in early adolescence were about being close to men and that those fantasies become eroticized in later adolescence. He told me that he and a neighborhood boy had indulged in a regular, if exploratory, sexual involvement when they were fourteen or fifteen.

When I asked him about heterosexual fantasies, desires, and experiences, he answered that he always had to force himself to think about women and summon from himself an erotic reaction. He had managed to contain the homosexual activity, had more or less placed it in a little compartment of his life, until finally he was diagnosed as progressively, developmentally ill. What hurt him was not the fact of his sickness but that it somehow rendered him unable to be generous or loving in what would be considered a normal relationship.

As he talked about his sexual struggle with women, I realized that he had been brightly animated and descriptive, even fervent, when he was talking about his attraction to men. Discussing women, however, he reverted to the humiliated, shamed demeanor that had so moved me when I first saw him. In what may have been a cruel test, I steered him back to the subject of men for a few moments, then back to women again, then repeated the switch once more. The change was sudden and profound, as if he had changed colors before my eyes. I was amazed that he did not seem to have any sense of it, that he appeared to not hear his tonal descent, his sudden abdication of gestures, as if his body had been numbed, his nerve endings switched off. I was watching a man become another man entirely, based on the focus of our discussion. This was not a man denying his heterosexuality, but a homosexual man who somehow did not know it.

When Roger talked of his real life, his true self, he was happy, fulfilled, and animated. When he spoke about the false life he had been trying so desperately hard to lead, he was humiliated and empty. He fled into his stories about his male–female relationships just as he must have fled into the relationships themselves, making his real sexuality shameful, secret, and isolating. He seemed perfectly oblivious to his changes and absolutely startled when I offered my reactions to what he had told me.

It was a sweeping intervention, despite the fact that I thought it obvious and simple; my therapeutic dilemma, however, was not so simple. I wanted to deconstruct Roger's illusion that he was mentally ill.

I said that in listening to his stories, I could state first that his therapist of seven years was a man loyal to his training. "But," I said, "given both your history and the current scientific convictions regarding homosexuality, you seem to me to fit directly alongside the many men who are biologically or genetically homosexual. There is nothing psychological about your sexuality. It is who you are, no more, or less. Your therapist, probably for the noblest of reasons, remained loyal to a long-held, carefully thought-out theory of homosexuality that has since been discarded as irrelevant and wrongheaded, though many therapists cling to it yet. Mistakenly, I believe, they equate what is quite healthy and natural with what is socially unadaptive and unhealthy. Traditional social convictions have condemned homosexuality throughout history, and if you think of the psychiatric establishment as among society's guardians, it makes sense that they would try to establish homosexuality as explicably and demonstrably wrong.

"But now we know that ten percent of every population is homosexual—every year, every decade, every century. Your memories of your physical attraction to men go back to age five, and that's without trying very hard to remember. There's nothing psychological about that. You are a statistical reality. How you handle it becomes more psychologically involved, but the fact is just a fact. You are a gay man. It is who you are, and no one has caused it.

"Here, try this," I said. "Just pretend for a minute that what I am saying is true, then we'll try to construct a psychiatric explanation parallel to your analyst's. If he had begun from my premise, here's what his theory might have looked like. If you are by nature gay, then your first erotic attraction would not have been to your mother; it would have been to your father. This is a little tricky, I know. It assumes that children have erotic attractions and that their parents are the first objects of their feelings. But if naturally heterosexual boys are attracted to their mothers, then it makes sense that naturally homosexual boys are attracted to their fathers. So, now, your father's alternating hostile or withdrawing behavior could have been his best means of dealing with what he sensed about you, about the nature of your different-ness, and it may have been designed to protect the relationship. Then, there could have been any number of reasons for the intensity of your involvement with your mother and for her soliciting such a close relationship with you. The first might have been simply that your father handed you off to her, in which case both of them would have been conspiring to protect you. Additionally, she may have felt some guilt about having produced a 'different' child, and some fear about how you would fare in a potentially hostile world when you grew up. She may not have framed different-ness in sexuality, but she surely knew that you were different. You remember her saying it, in fact.''

Roger was looking at me intently, bewildered, I think, at least at that moment, by what he took to be the enormity of the idea. For many people the notion of accepting their homosexuality is a colossal relief, because they have struggled with it for so long and read and heard so much about overinvolved mothers, exotically labeled complexes, damaged egos and libidos, and a whole spectrum of attempted explanations for this simple statistical fact. Roger was not relieved yet, though I suspected he would be. He said he felt very confused. "Everything is upside down," he said. I told him he probably had a lot to think about and advised him to go home and let these ideas percolate for a while. It still seems extraordinary to me that homosexuality may never once have occurred to him before, but he left in so blissful a daze that I remain convinced of it. Given his look of surprise, his system of denial must have been herculean.

Roger returned for the fourth session looking profoundly different. He gazed at me directly. For the first time someone had approved of him, and I think he felt somehow connected to me by that approval. His manner was animated again, though shaky, nervous. He even joked about himself, if cruelly. He said that he was surprised by the depth of his reaction. He spoke of how right it was beginning to feel for him, except that he also felt alternating waves of terror.

"On the one hand," he said, "I'm asking myself if I have led a totally mistaken life; then, if I've wasted my life; then, if I've even lived at all. And on the other hand, I don't know how to begin to live this other life. I fluctuate from feeling that this is right and perfect to feeling frightened to death. I mean, down to the details like how am I going to announce this to my girlfriend, let alone everybody else in my life? 'Hi, Joyce. Listen, the reason I haven't wanted to have sex with you lately is that you're a woman, see, and I'm gay. So I don't think it's going to work out with us. So long, and give a special hug to your brother for me.' Jesus! Even if I accept what you say about homosexuality—and in my head I think I do, because it makes such perfect sense, although sometimes I fluctuate there, too, and feel like I must be sick or depraved—but even when I agree, I'm no idiot. I know that the rest of the known world doesn't feel the same as you do. It strikes me like waking up black one morning in a white racist country. What difference does it make how right it feels? Most people are still going to hate me on sight. Then it goes back to feeling so perfect and natural again. To tell you the truth, I don't know who the fuck I am anymore. But I know I am terrified."

I told him I could appreciate both his terror and his sadness and anger about having spent so much of his life in this acquiscent denial. I said that many lesbians and gay men acquiesce to society's negative attitudes toward homosexuality—and for good reasons, at least on the surface of it. "Homosexuality does not appear to make sense," I said, "especially to someone who is not gay or lesbian. After all, if the entire species were homosexual, its perpetuation would be unpredictable at best. But most people, and by a wide margin, are heterosexual, so it's not a problem."

"So it is abnormal," he said. "You admit that."

"Well, if normalcy is statistical, you can probably argue that it's abnormal, but then you're falling into the trap of ascribing a level of value or quality to a fact that just is. Ten percent of the population is . . . whatever. Are they wrong? Should they feel shame for being? Should they not be? Can they not be? No. You were particularly vulnerable to feeling the shame because on top of all the societal pressure and the prejudice and the condemnation by religious traditions, you have a powerful tradition of shame in your family, one that has little or nothing to do with sexuality but that certainly would respond in mammoth ways to the idea of sexuality as shameful, as it evidently did, preventing you for all these years to recognize and accept yourself. Once you get used to that idea you will find that you will be able to live a well-adjusted and satisfying life, with a stable love relationship, if that is what you choose.

"Your analyst could not ever have predicted or assured you of that, because he did not accept the biology of your homosexuality. Therefore, he could not consequently view it as analogous to heterosexuality. So, from his faulty premise he constructed an analysis that searched for the environmental and familial causes of your homosexuality. That only served to enable you to continue this corrosive system of self-denial, easily accepted by you from those sympathetic traditions in your family.

"Your acceptance was so complete, it became an illusion. The illusion that you were sick rescued you, and in so many ways. It allowed you to remain loyal to all of these people in your life, to all the conventions and traditions they held dear, to the community at large, and even to the medical establishment. Under the illusion, your failures at relationships with women allow you to participate in the symptoms of your so-called 'sickness,' really your true self. But because in the illusion you view that behavior as failure, you continue to fail and continue to feel ashamed, and in so doing you continue to honor your father's perceived failures and shame.

"By embracing the illusion of mental illness, and keeping your shame both secret and shameful, you also continue to honor your mother's plea not to give your father any more to worry about than he already has. You don't reveal your secret 'mental illness,' so he is not hurt by that; and you don't surpass him in life, so he's not hurt by that. One final thing," I said. "My view, since I don't accept the environmental and familial factors of your homosexuality, since I accept it not as a preference but as a fact, is that your parents get neither the blame nor the credit for it. There is no credit or blame. Frankly, I think you should consider honoring your homosexuality. You would be honoring yourself."

In the following weeks and months, Roger seemed less interested in honoring his sexuality than in exploring it, and I had to caution him to slow down. The idea was not to try to catch up with what he'd missed in life. The idea was not even about sex, I told him, but about love.

"It has been the single most important fact in your life, because of all your years of self-denial and because of all your feelings of illegitimacy and shame over it," I said. "But it's not the single most important thing in life. It's going to be a slow process of unfolding and learning to honor yourself. It will likely be a roller coaster, sometimes torturously confusing and sometimes so exhilarating you'll fear you're going to explode with joy. You'll have to deal with your own negative attitudes that led you to turn away from yourself in the first place, and then, while you're struggling with that, you will be reminded of your place of rejection in the larger society. Eventually, if stability is what you choose, that is what you will achieve. What often has appeared to be the unstable gay life, which is the stereotypical view from the outside—the heterosexist view, in fact—is simply a matter of gay men and women who have no traditional maps to follow, basically navigating their lives in what turns out to be a unique, creative, and independent way. You'll learn to do that."

POSTSCRIPT

Here is a case that was infuriating initially for the cruel betrayal of an individual patient by the professional community and society at large, and then more cumulatively and retroactively, for the legion of similar betrayals it most assuredly represents.

For generations, gay people have been telling health and mental health professionals and whoever purported to represent society at large that the depth and the intensity of their feelings are so encompassing and, like any other biological feature, so much a part of their being that the feelings could not but be biological. Masses of gay people have said this over and over, pointing out the absurdity of the traditional psychological configuration. This assumed that an overinvolved mother and a distant father set up a context in which an individual was able to choose to be sexually attracted to persons of his own gender, when such attraction is manifestly involuntary. The fact is that gay men and lesbians come from so many different kinds of families that no explanation of parental involvement could possibly describe the creation of such a phenomenon. Plus, gay people have repeatedly reported that the attraction is strong universally at an early age. The persistent testimony of such a disparate environmental population, all over the globe and in every generation, suggests that a behavioral explanation of sexual preference is beyond being absurd and itself borders on the pathological.

But we have to remember that the psychiatric community is an extended family, and therapists are its members. Like family members, they are inclined to be loyal to tradition, to cling to family messages—even those that science has proven to be outdated, inaccurate, or simply impossible. The tragedy is that because of their loyal adherence to their professional family's wrongheaded past, the lives of a sizable portion of the population are lost and wasted.

This is the most maddening recurring theme among homosexual patients. A huge percentage of their suffering comes from professional and societal homophobia. And why not? If ninety percent of the population continually tells you that you are "deviant" by choice, you are likely to be affected. A good many of my cases have to do with homophobia that becomes internalized. In many cases, people accept as their own society's massive illusion that gay people can and should be changed.

Regarding the specifics of this case, a good part of the remaining therapy involved dealing with the inevitable field mines created by this internalized homophobia and its partner, shame. For Roger Birney, as is probable for every homosexual person, the future would be a lifelong daily process of nurturing self-confidence and self-esteem in the face of a gargantuan and pervasive illusion about one's real identity.

It had not yet happened that he felt very good about who he was, but when it did, he was sure to want to tell his parents, hoping for their acceptance, and like all of us, hoping to repair and then chance the relationship. In the meantime, life became easier for Roger as he embraced an identity, learned to practice safer sex and became integrated in the gay community which offered him solace, support, encouragement, entitlement, and an affirmative kinship system—which in turn enabled him to operate more confidently and openly in the larger, heterosexual world.

But, as always, it was an unnecessarily long road.

EPILOGUE

I've often wondered what would be a satisfactory semantic construction to describe my work. After identifying myself as a psychotherapist, what would I say I did? After offering my credentials, after saying that I had studied extensively the intricacies of human behavior and had obtained licenses to analyze and assist humans in behaving, how would I characterize my efforts? Did I "do" therapy, the way a cabinetmaker does carpentry? Did I "perform" therapy, the way an actor acts or a dancer dances? Did I "practice" therapy, as lawyers practice law, conceding uncertainty from the first? A public servant serves people. A doctor heals people. A cleric ministers to people. A teacher teaches them. What does a therapist do?

Reviewing, discussing, and compiling the stories in this book have helped me re-examine and redefine my life's work, which I consider an ever evolving art. Therapy is an extraordinary and continually reaffirming life experience, touched with magic and as much mystery as discovery. As a therapist, what do I do? I listen, see, perceive, sense, share, appreciate, respect, teach, escort, connect, risk, recommend, withdraw, watch, care, and learn. And then, marvel.

As simple as that.

The therapist's experience is one of incredible intimacy, which always occurs in episodic bursts. My experience sometimes seems even more intimate than that of many therapists, because in my departure from some of the more sacred rules of the trade, I allow myself to genuinely share and feel the emotional honesty my patients reveal to me: tenderness, joy, sadness, anguish, confusion, uncertainty, and love. I am moved by the depths of the experiences conveyed to me during a session, and I feel honored to have been asked to listen, privileged to have taken part, and reaffirmed when I feel that my intervention in a person's life has helped him alter his future in a creative and productive way.

A strange role, no question, especially in its touch-and-go aspects, where my wheels hit a life's runway, leave tracks, and fly off to the next appointment. Hour after hour, session after session, my patients, or clients, who in some instances evolve into my friends, share their most passionate and intense moments with me and then walk out my door, leaving me behind, as if I am to be unaffected thereafter by their fears, disappointments, and triumphs. I cannot be unaffected, of course. I do not believe anyone can; nor do I believe anyone should try to remain unaffected by such shared intimacy, passion, revelation, or truth.

I am moved and changed by each session with each patient. I think that every case a therapist ponders provides her with yet another perspective from which to confront some aspect of her own life and her own development. From that perspective, a given case can have a momentary, very immediate consequence for me, or it can become a transforming one for me.

In that way, I suppose, the story entitled ''Final AIDS'' has probably had the most profound and permanent effect on my life and my view of it. Choosing to work in the battlefields of the AIDS epidemic forced me to live more in the present, certainly. The enormity and intensity of the epidemic forced me to learn more about courage, uncertainty, insecurity, love, and letting go.

But my own life changed drastically after the experience in "Final AIDS." By that time I had spent years studying, training, learning, and improving my skills for whatever ambitions drive us to seek to achieve personal excellence and then reap such rewards and notoriety as accompanies it. Those two men taught me that in the face of death, only love had meaning. I'd heard love condemned by cynics as illogical or merely biochemical, as a phenomenon that often obstructs the positive development of a human being; I have yet to hear one cynic condemn love from his deathbed. In those moments that I talked with and observed the men in "Final AIDS," I saw that no amount of success, expertise, fortune, or status carried substantive weight at the end. At that point, what matters is only the answer to one question: who is this dying person loved by and able to love?

At the end of that academic year, I returned to New York. I re-ordered the way I worked and lived. I practiced less so that when I did work, I was at my most intensive. I became much more present-oriented and much less future-oriented. I did not return to the teaching institute, and I decided that more than any other goal, I wanted to live every moment as if I might not be entitled to another day. I was learning what the "Flirtations" sing: "The only measure of your words and deeds is the love you leave behind when you're gone."

Making those changes in my life seemed to have made me that much more resolute about telling these stories and writing this book. My perspective on the notion of change was significantly altered after the experience with such people as the couple in the story called, "The Immaculate Misconception." Therapy and life both speak to the constant balance of, on the one hand, staying comfortably and securely intact in life, loyal to the lessons of the past, and, on the other, of changing, presumably for the better. But change can never have a predictable outcome, and I have

long ceased trying to anticipate any. Cases like those described in the "Spaghetti Stories" taught me this truth early
in my education, and the lessons have grown broader and
deeper with every passing year. In "The Immaculate Misconception" case, I was extremely unsettled when I received the news, a year later, that the couple had embraced
and effected an enormous change in their lives. I had been
nearly rapturous in my admiration of the strength and spirituality it took for them to create the adamantine stability
they each so desperately craved. I was probably the first
person they had encountered who honored and admired
their marvelously unusual arrangement. Perhaps that admiration allowed them the freedom to move on, despite the
risks.

What consistently impresses me is the incredible creativity of the arrangements people make to repair and remain
loyal to the past while bravely facing the future. The way
people arrive at any solution to a problem is often infinitely
more creative than most of us could imagine and usually
offers a wider matrix of potential consequences than anyone
might predict—which is why many of the stories in this book
seem to have no particularly satisfying ending. The stories
really don't end, because the characters continue to reach
new impasses and must negotiate new choices for balancing
inertia and change—and with absolutely unpredictable consequences. I would not have predicted that the couple in
"The Immaculate Misconception" would have conceived
and birthed their own child, and I could never have predicted the potential consequences; certainly I could not now.
In fact, I feared the consequences at first. Then, much later,
I speculated that a couple strong and imaginative enough
to evade the risks of consummating their marriage might
actually have the strength and creativity to risk its consum-
mation. I will never know, of course, what precisely the
mechanism of change was, but the mystery never ceases to
amaze me and to inspire my imagination.

I would not have predicted that the man in the book's

title story, "The Patient Who Cured His Therapist," would break up with his girlfriend, though it makes sense to me in retrospect. I would never have predicted that the Irish couple in "The Wall of Sheets" would forever ritualize our admittedly unusual suggestion by periodically asking a priest to bless the sheets. I would not have predicted the decision to marry reached by the couple in "Double Cross," though I have often thought: what could be more generously creative than a man dressing up as his wife's twin, with extraordinary success, to spare her the agony of separation from her sister?

The constant and varied exposure to people's enormous talent and adaptability has created in me a sense of deep respect for the human ability to face problems and invent solutions. It certainly has stretched my level of acceptance of and affection for the world and its inhabitants, myself included. I have become much less judgmental in a qualitative-value sense and more of an appreciator in the manner of a member of an audience. I think for instance of the two men I mentioned in the introduction, who had in common the fact that they worried about the CIA monitoring their conversations through transmitters secretly implanted in their belt buckles. They might have scared me at one time in my life; my reaction to their illusions might have kept me distant from them. Now they fascinate me. I am awed by their adaptations and curious about the story that inspired it.

In order to practice, perform, or "do" therapy, I have to unravel not only the mystery of what I see in front of me, but my own feelings as well. In order to be honestly and genuinely empathetic, to relate on a deep emotional level, I have to reach into myself and search for a real experience that resembles the one being offered for examination. In order to emphathize with and describe the process of pain to, say, a patient struggling with a profound loss, I can summon vivid memories of my own pain and confusion during the process of my divorce. Having gone through certain experiences, I can feel confident about the evolution of pain, about the course it takes, and I can chart it. Knowing its evolution and its resolution, I am not frightened by it and can help the patient stand up to it. When I cannot recall a like experience, I must exercise an artistic imagination and create an emotional analogy that helps me better understand the situation. Some cases become part of the fabric of my life, especially those in which the experiences offered touch universal themes; others are unique and require a different kind of self-searching. They present a different and more creative challenge, and they add new dimensions to my development.

In terms of methodology, I have learned that my specific remedial approach usually falls into one of two broad categories. In one, interruption or intervention, I try to dislodge either the impasse or the accepted illusion—quite literally in the case of "The Immaculate Misconception," in "Sin's Syndrome," and in "The Patient Who Cured His Therapist," more figuratively in cases like "Jingle Jangle" and "Double Cross." In other cases, having discerned what is heroic in its accomplishment, I experience or develop a reverence for the problem. I do not know what makes me choose to feel or act one way or the other in a specific case. Much of my tactical behavior, on discerning a problem or a truth, seems to me to be instinctive and intuitive; I cannot determine whether I am acting or reacting at a given moment. Sometimes I see that a problem or a symptom or an illusion is so absurd that only an equally or more absurd action on my part will dislodge it and allow me to get to the real problem. Sometimes I am simply awed by the symmetry of the solution that has been mistakenly perceived to be a problem.

In re-examining my interventions, I notice that they tend to disrupt a pattern in order to create a certain confusion, which somehow requires that the principals resort to even more creativity than they already have exhibited. A more conventional therapy probably would prescribe a more normal way of behaving, whereas I no longer am looking for "normal" behavior. I prefer a more satisfying originality, which follows the patterns I have learned from my patients, an originality that allows people to continue to be loyal to their uniquely individual pasts without exacting such heavy consequences as they sometimes feel they ought to suffer. At the very least, they will accept that loyalty and generosity is what they are displaying, rather than neurosis and psychosis.

I am always conscious of shedding rules and conventions and of thinking creatively, conjuring more imaginative ways to live life. Life becomes more of an artistic creation as a consequence of therapy. In 1987, when I was first putting my ideas together with the idea of compiling this collection of stories, I wrote a note to myself about people's problems, about balancing change and instability. I wrote that people's definition of their problems tend to maintain the problems, and that the definition or perception has to be changed in order for the problem to be changed. In other words, change happens when people create a new balance.

Although I am fundamentally irreverent about the rules of psychotherapy, I do revere my patients' problems. Therapy is a circular process, and the therapist is as much a part of the process as the patient. Thus my life and my work are inseparable. My own life questions continue to draw me to the practice of therapy; my patient's questions attract me even more. We are all riddled with life's paradoxes, and we are always trying to solve them.

I sometimes have the ability to find the opening through which the sufferer can walk for that moment. I have been, I guess, what has variously been called a rabbi, priest, magician, and shaman. These are all extraordinary roles, but of course I am as ordinary as the patients who populate the stories. Simply put, I somehow have the ability to size up other people's situations in a moment of time—though, like them, I could spend a lifetime sizing up my own.

Thus, the stories in *The Patient Who Cured His Therapist* are about change, about transformation, about the avoidance and the acceptance of the consequences of either; about what may take place suddenly when what appears to be an old problem is cast in a new light; about what may take place gradually, in a process as simple and inexorable as growing older.

Stories teach us. Stories sustain and support us. And sometimes our interpretation of stories can ensnare us. As the details of integrated lifetimes accumulate to create a history, the characters in and from that history hold tenaciously to whichever interpretations of their story most comforts them. Now and then the interpretation creates or sustains an apparent problem. As I have learned, and as these stories attest, changing the meaning and the view of a story, of a past, of a family history, can provide a solid foundation for a new and more creative future.

ABOUT THE
AUTHORS

STANLEY SIEGEL

From his earliest memories of growing up in New York, Stanley Siegel recalls absorbing and recasting stories more by a visual understanding than by a verbal one. He preferred to use paintings, drawings, and choreographed visual depictions to the more symbolic, linguistic constructions to tell stories, to describe the relationships between people and objects, to explain the connections between people. When, as an undergraduate student, he elected to focus his energies on the study of psychology and human behavior, he found he could not shake his tandem interests in painting, sculpture, and dance. Ultimately he earned a dual major in psychology and fine arts, then a master's degree in art education, before returning to study human behavior and earn graduate degrees in social welfare and family therapy. He fervently believes that his studies in one field continually have inspired and challenged his proclivities and passions for the other.

After graduate school, Siegel studied under and practiced and then taught with some of the most renowned pioneers of family therapy. Now in private practice in New York City, Siegel, formerly a Senior Family Therapist and Director of Education at New York's prestigious Ackerman Institute for Family Therapy, has lectured extensively throughout the

United States, Canada, South America, Latin America, and Europe. He has trained mental health professionals of every discipline in his unconventional, tradition-challenging approach to psychotherapy. For three years, until he left his position as Assistant Professor of Social Welfare at the State University of New York at Stony Brook to join the Ackerman Institute, Siegel wrote a regular column called "Families" for the Long Island newspaper *Newsday*.

The father of a teenage daughter, Alyssa, herself an actress and a serious student of theater, Siegel lives on the Upper West Side of Manhattan and writes dance criticism for a New York entertainment weekly.

ED LOWE, JR.

Ed Lowe, Jr., left teaching in 1969 to begin reporting and writing for *Newsday*, currently the nation's fifth largest and fastest-growing daily newspaper. A columnist since 1977, he writes true stories from the lives of his readers.

In 1981, Lowe's work won the Mike Berger award from Columbia University Graduate School of Journalism. In 1982, 1983, 1985, 1986, and 1990, he received writing awards from the New York State Associated Press Association. And in 1983, his work was among three entries cited for writing excellence by the American Society of Newspaper Editors. Ed Lowe has taught advanced writing courses at Adelphi University and conducted writing seminars at the American Press Institute and daily newspapers, including *Newsday* and the *Richmond News Leader*.

A native of Brooklyn, and a nearly lifelong resident of Amityville, Long Island, Lowe is the father of two grown daughters and two young sons. At some risk, therefore, he also writes a twice-monthly essay for *Newsday* on "Fathering."